This is a refreshing study of the gre[...] and his grace. Dr. Nicole has the ab[...] attractive style and to deal with it in [...] will do much to recover the Reformation emphasis of the glory of God in every aspect of salvation; it will also help to dispel the myths of the modern church that the God of Calvinism has robbed us of the free offer of the Gospel, zeal for mission and assurance of salvation. On the contrary; as Dr. Nicole demonstrates clearly, only by recovering a sense of the greatness of the triune God, the definiteness of his atoning work in Christ and the nature of his decree, can we live meaningful lives of service to God in this world. This series of studies in theology is one of the most practical books I have read in a long time.

Iain D. Campbell
Back Free Church of Scotland

Over the years, Roger Nicole has proven himself to be a regular 'Mr. Valiant-for-Truth' when it comes to the Bible's precious teachings on the doctrine of salvation. Many of us have learned at his feet much about the meaning and significance of the atoning death of our Lord, about the doctrines of grace, and about the mystery of God's decree. These are but two reasons I am delighted to welcome the publication of these popular treatments of important biblical truths. Each chapter provides important material for practical Christian discipleship. Our salvation, our assurance of it, and our consequent growth in grace depend, in large measure, upon our grasp of the subjects he addresses here. May you become more deeply rooted in God's grace as you read!

J. Ligon Duncan, PhD
Senior Minister, First Presbyterian Church, Jackson, Mississippi,
Adjunct Professor, Reformed Theological Seminary

In an age when superficial preaching and superficial theology is filling churches with superficial Christians, we desperately need to rediscover the depth of God's truth in his Word. That depth of truth and corresponding depth of life has been captured nowhere more fully than in a Calvinistic understanding of Scripture. Although it has been maligned, misrepresented and rejected by many, Calvinism has brought a dimension into our understanding and experience of the Christian faith unrivalled by any other system of doctrine. In the pages of this book Roger Nicole brings us into the world of sane and satisfying Calvinism through cogent exposition, colourful illustration and compelling application. It will serve well as a primer for those new to the Reformed faith and as a refresher for those who know it well.

Mark G. Johnston
Grove Chapel, Camberwell, London

This is popular theology at its best. Nicole's addresses deal with the great doctrines of the faith in a thoroughly biblical way, always allowing the Word of God to speak for itself. The style is attractive and readily comprehensible, even when profound subjects such as predestination are under discussion. As a good teacher, Nicole is careful to stress the practical application of the truth – theology is to be lived out. These addresses will encourage, challenge and build up the people of God.

David McKay
Professor of Systematic Theology, Ethics and Apologetics
Reformed Theological College, Belfast

Our Sovereign Saviour

Roger Nicole

Christian Focus

In grateful recognition of my beloved wife
ANNETTE CYR NICOLE
who for more than fifty years
has been a loyal supporter
and an active participant
in all ministries God entrusted to me.
I gratefully dedicate this book to her.
Roger Nicole

ISBN 1-85792-737-0

Published in 2002
by
Christian Focus Publications, Geanies House,
Fearn, Ross-shire, IV20 1TW, Great Britain.

www.christianfocus.com

Cover design by Alister MacInnes

Printed and bound by Guernsey Press

Contents

Preface

The present volume, in contrast to *Standing Forth*, is made up of addresses to the general public rather than of essays written for a theologically trained leadership. Twelve of the fourteen chapters were in fact prepared for the *Philadelphia Conference for Reformed Theology*.

This yearly conference, organised with exceptional skill by Dr. James M. Boice, was developed in order to articulate in a winsome style the evangelical Reformed position on the major tenets of the Christian Faith. From the very beginning it met in the Tenth Presbyterian Church of Philadelphia, but branched out in addition to a number of different cities in the USA, up to three in a given year: Pittsburgh, Wheaton, San Francisco, Atlanta, Memphis, Seattle. Among the speakers, beside Dr. Boice and me, one could list Eric J. Alexander, William S. Barker, Edmund P. Clowney, John R. deWitt, Elisabeth Elliott, Sinclair Ferguson, John Gerstner, W. Robert Godfrey, Philip E. Hughes, S. Lewis Johnson, Jr., Ralph L. Keiper, C. Everett Koop, James I. Packer, Moishe Rosen, Stuart D. Sachs, Robert C. Sproul, John R.W. Stott and David Wells.

The conferences were taped, transcribed on the typewriter and then submitted to the speaker for corrections. Many of them were subsequently printed in a quarterly published by the Church: *Tenth*.

This explains the nature of the material presented in this volume. It will be apparent to the reader that an oral expression rather than a written text is the original source, in spite of some corrections that were fortunately introduced.

Since all my contributions were made prior to 1986, the frequent use of the generic sense of 'man' and of the masculine pronouns that follow will be observed. Since that time I have learned to be more sensitive to the expectations of many women, and I attempt to use forms of language that articulate inclusiveness rather than some that are too often construed as exclusive rather than generic. I apologize to my sisters for this: to attempt to correct this feature rather than reproduce the original text would have been a very burdensome task.

Since the volume was published in Scotland, the words like 'honor, color, Savior, etc.' are written in the British way with an additional 'u': 'honour, colour, Saviour, etc.' This does contrast with my ordinary diction, which reflects the fact that I learned English in the United States.

There are rather few footnotes or location of the origin of quoted material. The exception is in chapter 5, where the nature of the study would demand that a Biblical reference be indicated for each statement of Jesus. Even there, where more than one Gospel has recorded the statement, the location in Matthew or Mark alone is given.

It is appropriate at this point to express gratitude to Dr. Boice and those who worked with him to organise the conferences and prepare the material for the printer. My thanks also to Christian Focus Publications and its managing editor, Mr. Malcolm Maclean, for their initiative in publishing the book and their unfailing courtesy in the process. My gratitude to my wife, Annette, is indicated in the dedication of the book to her.

Roger Nicole

Acknowledgements

The chapters included in this volume appeared in other volumes and journals. Both the author and the publisher are grateful for permission to include them in this volume. The original sources are detailed below:

The Meaning of the Trinity: *One God in Truth*, eds. Peter Toon and James D. Spiceland, London, Samuel Bagster, 1980.

Soli Deo Gloria, *Tenth*, July, 1976.

Predestination and the Divine Decrees, *Tenth*, July, 1983.

Calvinism: The Five Points, *Tenth*, October, 1974.

Particular Redemption, *Tenth*, July, 1978.

The Doctrines of Grace in the Teachings of Jesus, *Tenth*, July, 1974.

Reconciliation and Propitiation, *Tenth*, July, 1978.

Justification: Standing by God's Grace, *Tenth*, July, 1980.

Sanctification: Growing unto God, *Tenth*, July, 1980.

Predestination and the Great Commission, *Tenth*, July, 1983.

When God Calls, *Equipping the Saints*, 1979.

Freedom and Law, *Tenth*, July, 1976.

Prayer: The Prelude to Revival, *Tenth*, July, 1982.

The Final Judgment, *Our Blessed Hope*, ed. J. M. Boice, (*Tenth*), Philadelphia, P.C.R.T., 1986.

1

The Meaning of the Trinity

The Christian Church readily acknowledges that the doctrine of the Trinity is a great mystery which has often been viewed as a stumbling-block, an obstacle in the path of those who would embrace the Christian faith, and a teaching so flawed by irrationality as to make it unacceptable to thinking minds. It is a major point of disagreement between Christianity and certain non-Christian religions, even those which, like Judaism and Islam, are ready to share a high degree of reverence for at least some portions of the Holy Scripture. A number of sects of Christendom have also found it desirable to repudiate the doctrine of the Trinity, and from within the ranks of the Church there have been questions about it and sometimes even attacks against it. It is therefore very important to define carefully the nature of the biblically based, orthodox view of the Trinity and to assess the impact of that view on the whole body of the Christian faith.

1. Definition
The Christian doctrine of the Trinity may conveniently be defined in three simple propositions, all three of which are concurrently affirmed.

1) There is one God and one only.

2) This God exists eternally in three distinct persons: the Father, the Son, and the Holy Spirit.

3) These three are fully equal in every divine perfection. They possess alike the fullness of the divine essence.

It is the Christian distinctive to affirm these three simultaneously. In fact, the most dangerous distortions that challenge the doctrine of the Trinity do affirm two out of the three and deny the third.

A. *Modalism* affirms that there is one God and that Father, Son, and Holy Spirit possess alike the fullness of the divine essence. It denies that God *eternally* exists in three persons. Rather it views the three as successive manifestations of one and the same person: God variously presented as Father or as Son or as Holy Spirit. Of course, this view is confronted by an immense problem in the many passages, particularly in the New Testament, where two or three persons of the Godhead are simultaneously present in the same incident. A good case in point might be the baptism of Jesus, described in Matthew 4 and Luke 4. There we have the Son who received baptism, the Father who speaks from heaven, and the Holy Spirit who descends like a dove. Other examples would not be hard to find. The very terms 'Father' and 'Son' imply a correlation which excludes unipersonality. In the earnest desire for stressing unity the modalist has done great disservice to the personal distinctions within the Godhead. The modalistic approach has been espoused by men of great intellectual power (Swedenborg, Schleiermacher, etc.) and appears to be perennially attractive to speculative thinkers.

B. *Subordinationism* affirms that there is one God but that three essentially separate persons must be considered when discussing our knowledge of God and of his relation to the world. What appears at variance with the Scripture is the proposition that the three – Father, Son, and Holy Spirit – do not possess alike the divine essence but that they form a hierarchy. Thus the claim of Jesus Christ to deity appears toned down and so is the deity of the Holy Spirit. Inasmuch as all three are to receive divine honours, there is here a very dangerous trend toward polytheism. An alternative consists in reducing Jesus Christ to the level of a mere man and in viewing the Holy Spirit as an influence, an expression of the person of the Father. Here obviously one is at great variance with the biblical representation. It is nevertheless in this category that the most common forms of Anti-trinitarianism can be classified. Arianism is the name generally used for this approach when conjoined with a recognition of high supernatural features in Jesus Christ.

C. *Tritheism* at another extreme asserts the eternal existence of the three and their full equality, but it denies the monotheistic doctrine of the uniqueness of God. On this account it could never be expected that tritheism would receive acceptance in the Church, since monotheism is deeply implanted in Scripture from Genesis to Revelation.

This situation may be depicted in the following diagram, where each side of the triangle represents one of the three propositional truths to be received. The orthodox view, represented by an inscribed circle, has a firm hold on each of the three great truths. The summits mark the respective positions of heterodox groups in which only two of the three truths are received and the third one is denied. It must be emphasised that this diagram does not constitute a schematic representation of the being of God; it is rather a diagram of the relationships between the trinitarian view and other positions.

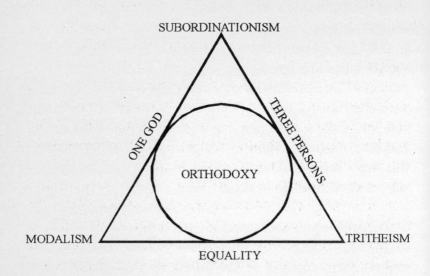

This diagram brings to light in a convenient way what orthodoxy would describe as the balanced nature of its own position. Moreover, it provides a ready explanation of the fact that often adversaries have confused orthodoxy with certain heretical positions. From the vantage point of a subordinationist, for instance, orthodoxy might be confused with modalism or with tritheism, because all three assert the full equality of the persons which subordinationism is concerned to deny. Thus Arius thought that Bishop Alexander of Alexandria was modalistic in his thought and expression. Arianism was in part a recoil against this putative danger. Similarly, a modalist may imagine that orthodoxy is either subordinationist or tritheistic. We are less concerned to trace out the misconceptions that tritheists may have, since they do not represent a significant movement within the Church.

It is important to recognise that the doctrine of the Trinity is a mystery. It is not, however, an absurdity, as some people have viewed it. Specifically, it is not asserted that God is one in the same respect in which he is three. What is propounded is that there is unity of essence, that this one essence is shared alike by each of the three persons, and that the three are conjoined in a total harmony of will and being, which far surpasses the unity observed between distinct individuals in humanity.[1]

In order to illustrate this truth, Christians of all ages have multiplied their efforts. Quite often, however, illustrations that have been offered are so far off the mark that they are injurious rather than helpful. For instance, it has been at times suggested that the three forms of water as ice, liquid, and vapour are representative of the Trinity. Indeed here we have a common chemical substance which, depending upon the temperature, takes varying physical forms. But this is illustrative of modalism more than it would be of the orthodox doctrine of the Trinity. Nothing here shows the interaction of the three in one. Under the circumstances it would seem that this illustration should be avoided because it may foster a wrong model. For the same reason the similes of the source, the rivulet, and the river, or the sun, the ray and the light, advanced by Tertullian (*Against Praxeas* 8), are to be adjudged very inadequate. Probably nothing that does not reflect some area of personality can be viewed as really appropriate.

Augustine in his great work *On the Trinity* has particularly explored the analogies between the Trinity and certain aspects of human psychological life. For instance, he analyses how love implies one person who loves, one other person who is loved, and love itself which binds these two. Similar analogies are found in the processes of knowledge and of consciousness. This approach may be seen as valid, as indicative of a certain mutuality in God, but as a mirror of the divine trinitarian nature it limps, since it involves two persons plus an abstract notion, rather than three persons, as would seem to be required for an adequate analogy.

In *The Secret of the Universe,* Nathan R. Wood has

explored in a most stimulating manner the question of the impact of the Trinity upon the structure of the world that the triune God has created. We cannot attempt here to give even a summary of the ideas contained in this book. Among the more meaningful parallels that Wood develops, one might mention three-dimensional space with its length, breadth, and height, or again time with its threefold components of future, present, and past. Here again personality is not a factor and therefore the illustration is wanting at a critical point; and yet the care with which the analogies are developed makes Wood's book especially arresting.[2]

In his work on the Trinity, de Margerie has focused attention particularly upon the family as a reflection of the trinitarian nature of God.[3] The advantage of an analogy which involves personality is obvious, but then the element of threeness does not appear indispensable, since a childless married couple do constitute a family and many families include more than three members. Probably it is wise to recognise that certain aspects of the Trinity may be reflected in a limited way in the created world, but that nothing reflects it in its entirety, precisely because it is the prerogative of God alone to be triune, and he shares with nothing else this particular distinctive.[4]

2. Impact
The impact of the doctrine of the Trinity on the Christian faith is very far reaching, for this doctrine fundamentally affects our understanding of God and of his relation to the world, particularly in terms of the redemptive purpose.

The doctrine of God is deeply affected by a trinitarian outlook since it represents God as possessing a sense of mutuality within his own being. The doctrine of the Trinity fosters an outlook upon God which emphasises life and movement within the Godhead. Without the trinitarian conception one could perhaps be embarrassed by the question 'What was God doing before he created the world?', for at this point the picture that would flash upon the screen would be that of a solitary being folded back upon himself and without opportunity for expressing in a meaningful way his life and perfections. God would then need the world in order to achieve self-expression and the independence of God would appear jeopardised. Of course, it might be thought that the question by its very nature transcends the power of our intellect and that we ought to be prepared therefore not to receive an answer that appears satisfactory to our minds. 'Here we have reached the limits,' we might say, 'and any attempt to proceed beyond this is doomed to failure from the start!' There may be some truth to the observation, and we do not presume here to assert that we are offering a full answer to the query. Yet the doctrine of the Trinity helps us to apprehend in God something of his own inner life, and to see in him the intimate attachment of the Father to the Son, of the Son to the Father, of both of them to the Holy Spirit, and of the Holy Spirit to both of them. This may help us to grasp how God is self-sufficient and how creation, involving as it does all three persons of the Trinity, was not, however, necessary for God's own existence or happiness.

When we discuss the activities of God, especially his redemptive activity, we may perhaps discern even more closely the paramount significance of the Trinity. It is especially important to confess that the one who offered himself as a ransom for many is none other than God himself, so that the price of our redemption has actually been paid by the Son's infinite offering of himself on the cross of Calvary. This is therefore not a third party who benevolently assumes by divine appointment the crushing burden that we cannot bear, and who is commissioned by the Father to do this in order that the indebtedness of men might be settled before his judicial throne. Rather, in the light of the doctrine of the Trinity we must see that in the person of Jesus Christ, God himself was incarnated, endured the full burden of our penalty and is therefore the proper basis for the redemption of anyone who is subsumed under him. The redemptive task was not accomplished by a third party entering the fray between the Father and the sinner, but it was the marvellous expression of the love and grace of the triune God, who in spite of the inexcusable character of man's offence, was gracious enough to provide a plan for salvation, to effect himself all that was necessary for the fulfilment of that plan (work of Christ) and to apply himself to the sinner the benefits which were secured by his own work as the incarnate Mediator (work of the Holy Spirit). In representing the Holy Spirit as the one who does regenerate, sanctify, seal, and glorify the redeemed, the Scripture continues to show that it is God himself who is at work in the redemptive process.

Alternative views, in which man is seen as not in need of any objective help to be brought back to God, or in which the help that man receives is conceived as proferred by someone else than God himself, are deeply unsatisfactory. They make a representation of God which must be rated very heinous, since he appears in the guise of a celestial Shylock who insists on reparations and accepts them from someone else. Or else they represent God as very lax and unwilling, or unable, to enforce his laws, so that one can apparently violate them without being at all punished. It is the doctrine of the Trinity which places this subject in the proper perspective. In Jesus Christ, the God-man, the love of the Father, the love of the Son, and the love of the Holy Spirit, as well as the justice of the Father, the justice of the Son, and the justice of the Holy Spirit are operative and manifested. To separate them here is to work incredible havoc in the redemptive purpose. And yet, it is here that most clearly within Scripture they appear as distinct. This may well be the reason why the Trinity was only faintly adumbrated in the Old Testament revelation and did find its supreme and definitive expression in the New Testament, after the incarnation and exaltation of the great Mediator, Jesus Christ, the God-man. Truly there is more at stake here than a mere vowel.[5] The whole structure of the redemptive plan is inextricably connected with the truth of the Trinity.[6]

Notes

1. The Trinity is presented as the supreme pattern for the unity of redeemed persons in the Church of God (John 17.11, 22f.; cf Eph. 4.3-6).

2. Nathan R. Wood, *The Secret of the Universe* (Fleming H. Revell, New York, 1932).

3. Bertrand de Margerie, *La Trinité Chrétienne dans l'Histoire* (Beauchesne, Paris, 1975), Bibliography, pp. 5-9.

4. A rather extensive discussion of the analogies of the Trinity, with an amazingly ample listing of suggestions proffered, may be found in H. Bavinck, *The Doctrine of God* (Eerdmans, Grand Rapids, 1951) pp. 321-30. (The original Dutch text, *Gereformeerde Dogmatiek,* 2nd ed. Kampen, Kok, 1908, II 332-41, has many references which are omitted in the translation.)

5. The fact that just one *iota* differentiated the words *homo-ousios* (of the same essence) and *homoi-ousios* (of similar essence) in the controversies of the fourth century led Edward Gibbon to sneer that the orthodox who were ready to die for the truth of Christ's deity were martyrs for a vowel's sake.

6. The following works, in addition to those referred to above, may be found useful in studying the doctrine of the Trinity: Millard Erickson, *God in Three Persons* (Baker, Grand Rapids, 1995); Francis J. Hall, *The Trinity* (Longmans, Green, New York, 1910) *(Dogmatic Theology)*; Pohle-Preuss, *The Divine Trinity* (Herder, St Louis, 1946) *(Dogmatic Theology* II); Peter Toon, *Our Triune God* (Victor, Wheaton, Il., 1996); T. F. Torrance, *Trinitarian Perspectives* (Clark, Edinburgh, 1994); Claude Welch, *In This Name: The Doctrine of the Trinity in Contemporary Theology* (Charles Scribner's Sons. New York, 1952); Herman Bavinck, *The Doctrine of God* (Edinburgh, 1977) Pp 255-334.

2

Soli Deo Gloria

In the triune God the three persons are concerned for one another's glory. The Son of God sought his Father's glory as he obeyed his Father's commands for his life on earth (John 7:18; 8:49-50). As he approached Calvary, his supreme desire was to glorify his Father, and he was assured that this would be the case (John 12:28). At the same time, in his knowledge of his Father's love, Jesus was confident that his Father would glorify him in his own right (John 8:50; 17:1-5). That confidence was fully justified. After Jesus had suffered, his Father gave him the glory for which he had prayed (Acts 2:32-33; 3:13). For his part the Holy Spirit is concerned for the glory of Jesus. He does not go off on some ministry of his own. Rather, he takes from the things that belong to Jesus and makes them known to his followers (John 16:14). We can also say Jesus is concerned for the honour of the Spirit. He prepares his disciples for the Spirit's coming and assures them that it is best for them that he leaves them (physically) so that they can begin to enjoy the Spirit's ministry (John 16:7).

If the persons of the Godhead are concerned for one another's glory, believers too should share this concern. All the more so, since our salvation is entirely of the triune God. At the Reformation they coined a motto – *Soli Deo Gloria*. Perhaps it is disconcerting that this motto is in Latin, but it is well known. It means 'To God alone be the glory'. *Soli Deo* – this is a dative in Latin – 'to God alone'. *Gloria* – 'the glory'. The Reformers were very eager to express themselves

with that word *solus*. They talked about the Bible alone –
sola Scriptura. They talked about faith alone – *sola fide*. They
talked about grace alone – *sola gratia*. And then they said,
'To God alone be the glory' – *Soli Deo Gloria*.

In a very remarkable way these words could stand as an
epitaph for one of the great leaders of Reformed thought,
John Calvin. Calvin has no epitaph because he has no tomb.
He had directed that when he would die his body should be
taken in a simple box of pine wood and be buried in
Plainpalais Cemetery without ceremony and without any
marker as to where his tomb might be. In some cases the
people of Geneva were not that eager to follow his leadership.
They gave him plenty of trouble during his life. But after his
death they managed to fulfil at least this request. So the place
where Calvin is buried is totally lost, and as a result, there is
no epitaph for Calvin. I would like to suggest that *Soli Deo
Gloria* might be a good epitaph for him because that was
veritably the master spring of his life. Here was a man who
was concerned not to gain anything for himself – in money,
fame, influence, affection, friends, or in any other way. He
was concerned only that the name of God be exalted, that
God's glory shine out in the city of Geneva that he had come
to love so greatly and beyond the walls of Geneva into that
devastated land of France from which Calvin came.

To this end Calvin exercised prodigious labours throughout
the days of his life. He did not allow himself to be stopped by
sickness. When he died he was suffering variously from gout,
rheumatism, an ulcer, colic, and recurrent headaches. But this
man, in spite of the weakness of health, problems in his family,
and the hatred and manoeuvres of enemies who were often
not at all particular about the methods they used – this man
continued to write, serve, preach (sometimes six times a week
and twice on Sunday), discuss cases, deliberate, govern,
organize and prepare the people of Geneva to magnify the

Word of God. So when at last, after fifty-five years of his life on earth, the Lord called him to his rest, it is, I think, proper to affix this epitaph to his life: 'To God alone be the glory.' Here was a man who was concerned to assert, develop, and exemplify in his life the sovereignty of God.

An inescapable doctrine

There are people who say, 'If you talk about the sovereignty of God, you are in danger.' And then, very quickly, the talk goes over into areas which are supposed to be obscure and very foreboding. There is the danger that one may begin to talk about 'radical corruption'. There is the danger that one may begin to talk about the 'definite purpose of God' in the death of Christ for those whom he planned to redeem. There is the danger that we may speak about 'judgment' and 'resurrection'. And all those things are not very palatable nowadays. 'Let us talk about things that are more suitable,' we are told. 'Let us talk about things that are more accessible, more winsome, so that our generation may be won.' But the Scripture does not seem to be concerned about these objections. I fully grant that we ought, whenever possible, to be winsome. There are no dividends in being more 'ornery' than we need to be. But our desire to be winsome gives us no right to modify or soft-pedal any element of the truth God has delivered.

When you open the pages of the Bible it is quite obvious that the Bible presents God as sovereign. And this is the great truth that the Reformers – and here not only the people of the Reformed Churches (not only Zwingli, Calvin, Farel, Beza and others which could perhaps be named) but Lutherans as well, and the Reformers of England – were very ready to acknowledge and emphasize.

When they said that God is sovereign they recognized that he is sovereign in the distribution of the knowledge of himself, in the impartation of his truth, so that the sovereignty of God leads to the recognition of an inspired Bible that is authoritative from cover to cover. It is not a mixture of errors and truths so that we have to go though the painful task of discerning the truth and rejecting the error. It is the Word of God which alone is able to give us guidance, which alone is able to provide for us the light that we need, which is the norm by which everything else must be judged and which no other norm can judge. Therefore the Reformers did emphasize the authority of Scripture; and they rejected, on one side, anything in the Roman Catholic tradition that tended to undermine or minimize the impact of this authority and, on the other side, the approaches of the enthusiasts and free seekers who thought they could take their pick among the things of the Bible, keeping what they liked and rejecting what they did not like.

When you talk about the sovereignty of God you also talk about a proper recognition of the supreme excellence of the triune God whose perfections are made apparent throughout the Scriptures, in nature, and particularly in the plan of redemption. Who speaks about the sovereignty of God must speak about God's justice, his holiness, his consummate love, his eternity, his immensity, his omniscience, about all the other dimensions of this prodigious being that we can only begin to understand when we yield our minds to the revelation of the Scripture.

The sovereignty of God has an impact upon our view of man. On the one hand, it lends dignity to man; for men and women are created in the image of God. Every member of the human race is the bearer of the image of the sovereign God, and on that account each is invested with infinite value far beyond anything that our material society can provide. On the other hand, recognition of the sovereignty of God implies that as his creatures we are obliged to conform to his commandments, that we cannot set forth for ourselves a system of ethics, rules and style of life which suits our fancy, that we are commanded to live under the sovereign command and authority of God himself. When this is recognized, then it is immediately apparent that God's standards are so high that none of us can possibly hope in any way to meet them. Thus, the sovereignty of God immediately crushes man as sinner into the very dust of the ground, for he is unable to rise in God's presence but must be the object of his fearful condemnation.

When we speak about the sovereignty of God we speak about God as sovereign in the plan of redemption. Jesus is not some man who merely hoped to be acceptable to God, not somebody who (like other men or even more than other men) had a consciousness of the divine, but God himself, God the Son coming down to our earth to share in our situation, take upon himself the burden of our sins, and bring us redemption. No one but God himself could work that out for us. God in Christ bore the awful burden of our penalty in its fullness in order that we might be liberated from the terrible guilt of our sins before the judgment bar of God, so that we may be redeemed, washed and justified in the presence of God and rejoice in the blessings that he has provided for those who belong to him.

When we talk about the sovereignty of God we emphasize the sovereignty of God the Holy Spirit who works in the lives of men and does not await some consent that would be coming from unregenerate sinners but who himself transforms at the very depths of their personality lives that are disrupted, distorted and destroyed by sin. He plants within the very heart of sinful man the principle of a new life and reorganizes, reorients, reforms and renews in every possible way that which sin has demolished, destroyed and damaged. This Holy Spirit in his gracious mercy does not only originate new life, he develops, nurtures, seals, and preserves it for the final day of fulfilment. Even at death he completes his work in the soul, and at the time of the resurrection he perfects the work in glory for the redeemed, who are then fully renewed in the image of Jesus Christ.

When we speak about the sovereignty of God we speak of his sovereignty in the life of the Church, in the life of God's people who do not have simply a society or organization of their own devising but who are gathered together under the guidance and leadership of God himself speaking his word and moving by his Spirit. We speak of God who works through sacraments, the sacraments that he himself has established and instituted, whose number has been determined by him, and whose form has been communicated to us. Their efficacy is controlled by him. Their administration must be in accordance with his Word. Their blessing is enjoyed when there is an obedient acceptance and reception of that which he himself has prepared.

When we speak of the doctrine of the sovereignty of God we recognize that he will be sovereign at the last day. This is a sovereignty that has its beginnings in eternity past, that carries through the long and checkered history of mankind and that will not abate at the last. For at the last day the power and the glory of God will be made manifest. Then he will sit on the throne of judgment to manifest his glorious justice in the condemnation of those who are rightly condemned for their sins.

There is no place in theology where the sovereignty of God has not its impact. There is no place in theology where we can say, 'Here I can forget about it, and I can move along other lines.' The sovereignty of God is like a ray of light which permeates the totality of the theological enterprise. Therefore it is very appropriate that we should concentrate our attention on this great theme in this chapter.

Immorality checked[1]

But then objections arise. Some argue, 'All this sounds good (or perhaps does not even sound so good), but is it really possible? Can we really hold any view like that? If we say that God is sovereign, what will happen to morality? If we say that man cannot under any circumstances produce good works so that there are really no ultimate differences between actions, does that not wipe out from the very start the whole principle of distinction between good and evil among men? Does that not make morality impossible?'

Well, I suppose one could proceed to discuss this matter in a theological manner – to examine arguments, consider objections, and line up points in an orderly disposition. I would like, however, instead of going into a theological discussion, to challenge you in terms of an historical consideration. In the Reformation, we have a group of men who made precisely these assertions. Over against the prevailing current, they said that man is radically corrupted and is therefore totally unable by himself to please God. He is incapable of gathering any merits, let alone merit for others. But did this in fact damage morality? Were these people a group of scoundrels who satisfied their own sinful cravings under the pretence of giving glory to God? One does not need to be well versed in church history to know that this was not so. There were thefts, sexual sins, dishonesty in the sphere of government and politics, murders, unjust wars. Even within the church there was a heinous and shameful trafficking of sacred positions. But what happened? These people, who believed that man is corrupt and that only God can help him, came forward like a new breath of air. They brought in a fresh recognition of the rights of God and of his claim upon the lives of men. They brought in a new chastity, a new honesty, a new unselfishness, a new humbleness, and a new concern for others. 'Honest like the Huguenots,' they used to say. In some cases, when tempted to free themselves from great difficulties by lying, they would not perjure themselves but stuck to the truth even to death. Immorality was not promoted; it was checked by the recognition of the sovereignty of God.

'It is impossible,' some say. But that is what happened.

True freedom

Others say, 'If we assert that God is sovereign, this will make freedom impossible. It will encroach on the proper sphere in which man has to exercise his own activity, his power of making choices, and his sense of responsibility before God. If God has decided everything, man is reduced to the level of being a puppet or a robot.' Now I do not know if there is anything so fearfully bad about puppets and robots. I suppose in their place they have their value. But surely all of us would agree that this is not the place which God has provided for men; and so, if men and women are reduced to be puppets and robots, then we have made a serious departure from the biblical representation of man.

But again, rather than going into the arguments of the matter, let us merely examine what happened in the sixteenth century when the sovereignty of God was once again asserted. Did the people involved allow themselves to be robbed of all initiative or were they ones who sensed an enslavement under the power of God? Not at all! On the contrary, they were people who were very keenly aware of their responsibility. They had the sense that for everything they were doing, saying, and thinking they were accountable unto God. They lived their lives in the presence of God, and in the process they were pioneers in establishing and safeguarding precious liberties of all types – liberty of speech, religion and expression – all of which are at the foundation of the liberties we cherish in the democratic world. Far from eclipsing their sense of having freedom, true proclamation of the sovereignty of God moved them toward the recognition and expression of all kinds of human freedoms which God has himself provided for those whom he has created and redeemed.

'It is impossible that this should happen,' we are told. Perhaps! But it happened!

Vigorous activity
People also say, 'If you teach the doctrine of the sovereignty of God – that God directs and appoints everything, decreeing whatsoever comes to pass, as the Westminster divines were later led to express it – this is going to ruin the whole value of human activity. There is no point of exerting yourself in any way.' From this perspective, recognition of the sovereign super-intendence of God seems to be in conflict with the significance and value of human activity.

But again, we may make an appeal to history. What did these people – Calvin, Farel, Knox, Luther – what did they do? Were they people who reclined on a soft couch saying, 'If God is pleased to do something in Geneva, let him do it. I will not get in his way.' Or, 'If God wants to have some theses nailed to the door of the chapel of Wittenberg Castle, let him take the hammer. I will not interfere.' You know very well that this is not so. These were not people who were lax in renouncing their activity. They were not abdicating from their responsibilities as God's instruments. They were not lazy. Calvin may be accused of many things, but one thing he has seldom been accused of is being lazy. One would, I think, have to be very bold to come forward with an accusation like that. No, when the sovereignty of God is recognized, then meaningfulness comes to human activity. Then, instead of having our efforts seen as the puny movements of insignificant people who cannot resist the enormous momentum of a universe that is so much larger than ourselves, we see our activity in the perspective of a sovereign plan in which even small and insignificant details may be very important. Far from renouncing activity the doctrine of the sovereignty of God has been a strong incentive for activity, labour, devotion, evangelism and missions.

'It is impossible,' but it has happened anyway!

God's men, God's women
In the first century the world was in a frightful condition. One does not need to be a great authority in Roman history to know that. There were signs of the breakdown of the Roman Empire – a dissolution of morals, the invasions of barbarians, hedonism. But at that point God was pleased to send into the world that great preacher of the sovereignty of God, the apostle Paul, and this introduced a brand new principle into the total structure. It did not avert the collapse of the Roman Empire, but it postponed it. Moreover, it permitted the creation of a body of believers that persisted even through the Dark Ages and the terrible invasions of the barbarian hordes.

At the end of the fourth and the beginning of the fifth centuries the threat was perhaps even more serious, for now paganism had crept into the church. Pelagianism reasserted the claims of man – man capable, sufficient, able to help himself, from whom God could not require anything more than he was able to accomplish. But at that point God raised for the defence of the truth that great servant of his, that great preacher of grace, Augustine of Hippo, the most influential man between the apostle Paul and the present time. Here again it did not dispel all clouds; it did not avert all the shipwrecks of individuals or even of churches; but in the presence of the monstrous threats of humanism, even within the church, it safeguarded the truth of the gospel centred in the grace of God and his sovereignty.

In the sixteenth century, once again the church had

succumbed to deep corruption. It was corrupt in its head and members. At many points it was a cesspool of iniquity. People did not know how to remedy the situation. They tried councils, internal purges, monastic orders. None of these things seemed to work. But God again raised up to his glory men who proclaimed the truth of his sovereignty, the truth of God's grace. In proclaiming this truth they brought out a multitude of the children of God into a new sense of their dependence upon and relationship to Christ. In proclaiming this truth they benefited immensely even the very people who opposed them in the tradition of the church. They were small, these men of the Reformation. They had little money, little power, little influence, as it would seem. One was a portly little monk in Germany. Another was a frail little professor in Geneva. A third was a ruddy but lowly little man in Scotland. What could they do? In themselves, nothing. But by the power of God they could shake the world.

Radically corrupted, but sovereignly purified!
Radically enslaved, but sovereignly emancipated!
Radically unable, but sovereignty empowered!

These men were the blessing of God for our world.

Today we face a similar situation. Today there are also everywhere the signs of disillusionment and of collapse. There are threatening clouds on the horizon. There are threats without and within. There is a frightful degradation of morals and lowering of life. May God raise up men and women who believe in the sovereignty of God and who proclaim it and live it! The world needs them now!

Notes

1. The end of this chapter is practically a free translation of Emile Doumergue, 'La souveraineté de Dieu,' in *Etudes et Conférences*, Vauvert Gard, Union des Chrétiens Evangéliques, 1929, pp. 15-18.

3

Predestination and the Divine Decrees

Some people do not like talk of predestination. They feel it is at best irrelevant and at worst harmful to the believer. Yet, if our ambition is to glorify God, predestination is far from irrelevant. It is of the utmost importance to know what is the source of our salvation. Was it a plan of the triune God from all eternity? Or was it some improvisation from God to deal with the realities of human sin?

In fact, Scripture makes it clear that predestination is but one chapter in the more encompassing book of the sovereignty of God. For the doctrine of divine decrees recognizes that everything that happens (and not merely the salvation of some women, men and angels) takes place at God's command. The sovereignty of God encompasses all events in the unfolding history of the universe. That includes predestination, involving the purpose of God for the salvation of certain individuals whom he has chosen. If we are to give God the glory that is his due, we ought to recognize predestination as part of the outworking of his sovereign control of the universe.

The Westminster Confession of Faith (III,1,2) articulates very beautifully the all-embracing nature of his sovereign will

> God from all eternity did, by the most wise and holy counsel of his own will, freely and unchangeably ordain whatsoever comes to pass: yet so, as thereby neither is God the author of sin, nor is violence offered to the will of the creatures, nor is the liberty or contingency of second causes taken away, but rather established.

Although God knows whatsoever may or can come to pass upon all supposed conditions; yet hath he not decreed any thing because he foresaw it as future, or as that which would come to pass upon such conditions.

This statement presents six positive features of the decrees of God. Then it provides a caution against four possible misunderstandings.

Positive features

The decrees of God are characterized by the fact that they are God's decrees; they participate in the nature and perfection of God himself. Therefore, the first thing to be stated is that the decrees are *eternal,* as God is. God does not have to be making up his mind constantly but rather from all eternity has made a plan and purpose. The purpose of God is not related to time or affected by adjustments to events that occur. There is no way of saying, 'What did God do before he made this plan?' There is no answer to such a question, because there is no 'before' eternity. True, the execution of God's plan takes place in time, but the establishment of his plan is eternal, as God is.

This is apparent in Ephesians 1:4 where we read that God 'chose us in him [Christ] before the creation of the world.' This dispels misunderstandings, because there are people who think, for instance, that God had to wait until Adam fell before he could articulate predestination, and that the decree of salvation took place after the fall of Adam and Eve. No one who is a proper Calvinist affirms that, for the decrees of God are eternal and thus whatever happens was decreed from eternity.

Second, we read that God made his decrees 'by the most… wise counsel of his own will.' This affirms that the decrees participate in God's *wisdom.* This is also important, because there are people who think (because we do not know all the reasons that led God to decide something) that God's decisions are arbitrary. This often occurs when a clear presentation of the doctrine of gracious election is given. When we state that there is no preferential feature in the elect that caused God to choose them, that they are not in themselves preferable to the non-elect, these same people sometimes draw the inference that the choice of God is therefore arbitrary. It is a choice at random. It is not worthy of God. In answer we must insist that every decree of God is wise. It is not necessary for us to see wherein his wisdom consists in order to assert it. For that is precisely the faith to which the Christian is called: to recognize the wisdom of God even though he may not perceive how this wisdom functions.

This was the case with Job. He could not understand why God permitted the series of catastrophes in his life. Yet in spite of his ignorance he recognized that God is the ruler and that in some way wisdom was at the root of what God was doing. This was shown to him in a stunning manner by the questions God asked (found in chapters 38-41). These chapters stress the importance of trusting God even though we do not perceive how his wisdom is functioning in certain events.

Third, the decrees of God are *holy*. God decreed from all eternity by the most wise 'and holy counsel of his own will.' The purpose is one in which God does not put himself under responsibility for evil. He does not besmirch his holiness by having made the plan he did. This is more specifically articulated in the first misconception noted in the sentence that says that God is not made thereby the 'author of sin.' That same truth would be expressed in saying that the counsel of God is holy. There is no way in which the holiness of God will be impugned by the decrees when they are properly understood. On the contrary, the decrees of God, particularly the decree of predestination, are designed to lead us to holiness and not to abandon us to a life of profligacy and disorder.

Fourth, we are told that the decrees of God are *free.* That is, there is no external power over God which compels him to decide or ordain anything. God is not moved by external powers which somehow make the decree inevitable. It is in his own sovereign freedom that God ordains and purposes whatever he has planned. This freedom is the freedom of God, and the freedom of God is qualified by the beautiful things we read in Scripture about his nature. The character of God articulates what he will determine in his freedom – in the same way our character determines what we decide when it is given to us to make decisions. However, there is nothing outside God which obligates God to decide one way or another. The decree of God is a sovereign decree in which he stands at the very peak of the pyramid. There is nothing above him to oblige him one way or the other.

Fifth, the decree of God is determined 'unchangeably.' It is *immutable.* We can understand very readily how this must be if we ask the question: What would cause God to change his mind? Most of our decisions are changeable, because there are events over which we have no control. When these occur we should be willing to change our minds. People who never want to change their minds are playing God, and playing God is a very dangerous game both for ourselves and others. Our minds must be mutable because we can err or be overtaken by situations beyond our control. But what in the world would cause God to change his mind? Certainly there is no unforeseen development which would suddenly call for a shift. God is omniscient and therefore knows everything that will happen. There can be no unexpected development for God. Furthermore, when God first made up his mind he did it in light of the fullness of his own being. So there is no preferential option to be chosen. From the start God chose the option which is supremely good, wise and acceptable in his own sight.

Sixth, it is stated that God has ordained 'whatsoever comes to pass,' so that the decree may be called *all-encompassing.* There is nothing in the whole world which is not included in God's purpose.

This 'blows our minds,' so to speak, because we function with severe personal limitations and therefore often cannot be bothered with small details. God is not like us at this point. God is so great in his governing ability that he takes account of even the smallest details of running the universe. No one expressed this more forcibly than the Lord Jesus himself, when he said that even the flights of little sparrows are part of God's purpose. 'Not one of them will fall to the ground apart from the will of your Father' (Matt. 10:29). In the same passage he also said that the 'hairs of our head are all numbered.' This seems to be irrelevant. Besides, this number fluctuates. Why in the world would God take account of this? The point of our Lord, as I understand it, is to show us that we cannot mention anything, be it ever so minute and apparently irrelevant, over which God does not maintain a perfect control so that, as we said, his decree encompasses 'whatsoever comes to pass.' This is tremendously encouraging for those who know the Lord as Saviour. There is no circumstance of life that should be totally disconcerting, because God has ordained it and is at the back of it. His loving and gracious purpose is fulfilled even in events which may appear quite contrary to our wishes.

Four safeguards

Having described the decree by six positive statements, the Westminster Confession now adds safeguards against four possible misunderstandings.

First, *God is not the author of sin.* We recognize that sinful acts are encompassed in his total plan, but God is not himself the first cause of evil in them. The evil has to be adjudged in terms of another source or causation. This baffles us tremendously, as anything connected with evil ultimately does. The Synod of Dort, which met about thirty years before the Westminster Assembly, put it in an even more forceful manner. They said, 'By no means is God the author of evil, the very thought of which is blasphemy.' They did not mean that their adversaries were blaspheming by presenting this objection. They meant that if somebody seriously entertains the thought that God is at the root of evil, and believes that, he besmirches the holiness of God. That is where the blasphemy occurs.

Second, the Confession says that *violence is not offered to the will of the creature*. Many have reasoned that, if God has ordained everything, no room is left for human or angelic freedom. Creatures become robots that fulfil mechanically what God himself has appointed. If that were true, it would undermine the sense of responsibility which we as human beings ought to have before God. But the Westminster Confession is careful to say, 'We don't want to imply this at all. We want to recognize the sovereignty of God, but we want also to assert that the wills of the creatures function.'

Third, it is stated that *the liberty or contingency of second causes is not taken* away, but rather established. That is, God does not ordain things simply 'out of the blue,' so that history is only a conglomeration of unrelated events having no connection with one another. Rather, God has ordained things in a texture, so to speak, so that everything that happens is related to everything else. That God has decreed what happens ought not to be interpreted as implying that he has decreed anything independently of that by which he makes it happen.

If I lift up a book, I can know that God has ordained that it should be raised. I know that because it is raised. There it is!

But notice, it has to be raised by my hand. If my hand did not raise the book, it would stay where it was before I raised it. The purpose of God which involves the lifting of the book also involves the means by which this lifting occurs. You cannot disconnect the effects from the causes. So the liberty or contingency of second causes is not taken away, but is established, because it is God himself who has made the principle of effectuation function in the universe. It is by God's appointment that causes produce effects. Therefore the decree must be understood in line with the total order which God has established in the world.

Some people misunderstand what is at stake here, saying, 'There is no sense in going to the mission field, because if the heathen are elected, God will save them anyway, and if they are not elected, our going will not help.' As a result of this erroneous thinking some people believe that Calvinism is opposed to evangelism and missionary zeal. This is a grievous distortion and a serious charge. It fails to see that God does not ordain things without the means whereby they take place. Specifically, he does not ordain the salvation of people without the preaching of the Word (at least for those who reach the age of accountability). He does not ordain the blessing of the soul without the means whereby the soul is blessed. He does not ordain that your life is going to be nurtured unless you cling to Jesus Christ and have recourse to the means of grace. The means are part of the plan of God, and it is impious to disconnect the ultimate purposes from the means God has chosen to achieve those purposes.

Fourth, there is the statement that *the decrees of God are not grounded in his foreknowledge.* This is to counteract the Arminian assertion that God has made a plan involving everything that happens but that he made it in view of whatever he foresaw people would do. Specifically, he decreed that some would be saved because he foresaw that these would have faith. Here the Westminster Assembly was careful to assert that the decisions of God are not grounded in foreknowledge in the sense that God saw in advance what would happen and therefore said, 'Okay, let it happen,' but rather are sovereign decisions which God has taken in and of himself, which are not based on the advance knowledge he has. If the decree of predestination was grounded in foreknowledge, it would be disastrous for us. For how could God foreknow anything good about us apart from the grace he gives? What we need in the first place is to receive grace so that we can believe. This is how the Calvinist views the matter.

People say that Romans 8:29 does seem to teach that predestination is grounded in foreknowledge: 'For those God foreknew he also predestined to be conformed to the likeness of his Son.' But here the word 'foreknew' is used in the biblical sense of 'love in advance,' 'choosing in advance,' not simply to have advance information. It is perfectly obvious that if God simply has advance information about what we might do, then the information would be that all of us would be lost. None of us would respond to the invitation of his grace. In order that the purpose of predestination should be fulfilled, it is necessary that the Holy Spirit be active within our hearts to move us to respond, to change our wills and the dominant disposition of our natures, and thus enable us to repent and believe. This is articulated more fully in other chapters of the Confession, but it is anticipated in that second paragraph of chapter 3 where the ground of the decrees is presented as God's sovereign free will.

The order of God's decrees
What about infra- and supralapsarianism? The issue arises from attempts to order God's decrees, particularly those related to salvation. How are the decrees related to one another?

We begin by noting that this is not a matter of chronological order. Since the decrees are eternal, distinctions of time are not valid at this point. What is asked is: How is the plan of salvation expressed and articulated? Some have said, 'The very first thing we must recognize in the plan of God is his desire to have some people in whom the sovereign beauty and glory of his grace will be made manifest and other people in whom the sovereign glory of his justice will be made manifest.' This would be the foundation idea on which God would proceed, according to this view. In order to have these people God would then say, 'Well, I need to create them. But also, in order to have an opportunity to manifest both grace and justice, they need to be permitted to fall.' After this the purpose of redemption would come, in which God would send his Son to be the redeemer of those whom he has appointed to glorify him in grace. In the end he would decree to send the Holy Spirit to move these people to repent and accept the offer of salvation presented in the name of Jesus Christ. This is the supralapsarian order.

Supralapsarianism sounds very difficult, but it is really not hard to understand. In Latin *lapsus* means 'fall.' (Sometimes people talk about a *lapsus linguae* when somebody gets tongue-twisted in pronouncing something.) *Supra* means 'before' or 'preceding.' So supralapsarian simply means that in God's mind the decree to elect some and reprove others precedes the decree to permit the Fall. The decree to permit the Fall is an articulation of the purpose to have people saved to magnify his grace, and to have some people lost to magnify his justice.

Over against this view infralapsarianism states that in God's mind the decree to choose some and bypass others comes after the decree to create man and permit the Fall. According to this order, the very first thing God would decide (logically, as it were) is to have a race of humanity bound together by the bond of the covenant of works and then to permit the fall of that humanity through the persons of our first parents, particularly Adam. Then in the presence of this great mass of misery God, instead of confining all to damnation as we deserve, chooses in his mercy to save a great multitude, who are the elect, and to bypass others, permitting them to receive the punishment due them for Adam's and their own sins. The other two decrees, to provide salvation by Christ's death and to apply salvation by the Holy Spirit, then follow in logical order. In order to have an elect body, redemption would be provided in Jesus Christ. In order for this redemption to be effective, the Spirit would apply it to the elect. Thus we would have five decrees, in that order.

Some people have felt that this whole matter is idle speculation, since we have no way of going into the mind of God to try to establish this order. We remember that Calvin strongly condemned speculations which have no real basis in Scripture. Yet I think, in spite of this objection, that the issue is important for the way in which the plan and blessings of salvation are presented. This is made apparent in a beautiful little book written by B. B. Warfield entitled *The Plan of Salvation.* He shows that Calvinistic, Lutheran, Arminian and sacramentalist points of view originate in different understandings of the nature and order of God's decrees.

Supralapsarianism

Which of these views – supralapsarianism or infralapsarianism – appears to be more appropriate? The great advantage of supralapsarians is that they manifest the purposive nature of the divine plan even with respect to the Fall. The purpose which comes into fulfilment at the end is also the very same as God had at the beginning. This has been presented in a rather stunning manner by Gordon Clark who is a strong supralapsarian. He says that where you have purpose, the order of that purpose is always the reverse of what transpires in history. Suppose that my purpose is to give a lecture at the Philadelphia Conference on Reformed Theology. I know that to give this lecture I will need to take a plane from Boston to the conference city. In order to take the plane I will need to drive my car to the airport. In order to drive my car to the airport I will need to leave my house at a certain time. The order of purpose is: 1) getting to the location, 2) taking the plane, 3) driving my car, and 4) leaving my house at a particular moment. But what happened in history? At the appropriate moment I left my house, drove my car, took the plane, arrived at the conference and am now giving the lecture. The purpose is mirrored in history, in reverse.

Of course, our lives are not wholly integrated. Our purposes change, and new purposes originate. We do not have a purpose that can be analysed readily. But God has a totally purposive outlook. Therefore, everything that happens reflects backwards (in order) what he intended in the first place. In view of this we ask: What will happen at the end time? The answer is that God will have great multitudes who are saved and other multitudes who are lost. This will be the closing scene. Therefore, Clark would say, the very first thing that God intended is that. The last thing he intended is creation, because creation is what happened at the beginning of time.

Well, there are difficulties in this. The first is that we cannot see how people can be saved who are not even viewed as existing. The decree of salvation seems to have no content. And if the decree has no content, then it has no significance either. A decree must be a decision to act, and you cannot decide to act when you do not have a content for the action. The idea of creation seems to be essential for a decree to be rendered.

Again, the order in which saving events occur is not as simple as the mere reverse of the order of history. I can show this in terms of the relation of Abraham to the work of Christ on the one hand, and of John Calvin to it, on the other. Historically they are on opposite sides of the cross. Yet in terms of salvation they are related to the cross in exactly the same way. If the supralapsarians are correct in ordering the decrees by a backward unrolling of history, then everybody who is saved should be on the same side of the cross – but this is not the case.

Supralapsarianism also gives the impression that God condemns some people arbitrarily, without their having done anything worthy of condemnation. So at this point it puts more venom than is necessary into the doctrine of reprobation. Reprobation is always condemnation for sin.

Infralapsarians

But infralapsarians have a problem also. The problem they have is in showing the purpose of the first two decrees. According to their view, God seems to be creating in a void, without having anything that he particularly plans to do, and then permitting the Fall without a purpose. In the presence of the misery of sin he would then respond by electing some in his great mercy and by bypassing others.

Infralapsarianism does have an advantage in two things. First, it emphasizes that we are elected in Christ, and obviously Christ has come into the world in relationship to the predicament of misery and sin already viewed in God's mind. Christ is the Lamb of God, slain from before the foundation of the world. Election is in Christ, because it is in relationship to this tremendous purpose that God has chosen a multitude whom he has been pleased to plan to redeem.

Second, the infralapsarian view also points to the fact that election is out of the mass of perdition. It is not just an arbitrary determination of destinies. Rather, the elect are viewed as among the mass that deserved the just judgment of God but who are rescued from it by the immense mercy and grace of God the Father, God the Son, and God the Holy Spirit. The Father plans their salvation; the Son effects it; and the Holy Spirit applies it. Since many scripture passages present a common mass of perdition out of which some people are chosen, the infralapsarian seems to have some biblical advantage at this point.

It is not absolutely necessary that we should opt for one or the other. There are people who live contented lives without thinking about these particular subjects. But when we deal with the doctrine of the decrees, these questions arise and it is important that we deal with them as carefully as we can.

4

Calvinism: The Five Points

The five points of Calvinism are major distinctives of the Reformed faith. They aim to give God the glory that is his due as our sovereign Redeemer. They also aim to strengthen the people of God and to enable them to walk within the paths of righteousness. However, these points come to us today in a form that is quite traditional: total depravity, unconditional election, limited atonement, irresistible grace and perseverance of the saints. But we are not to think that this is the only form the doctrines of grace can take or that the phrases themselves are unalterable. The advantage of this particular formulation is that when you take the first letter of each of those points and read it from top to bottom you find the word 'tulip' and so have an acrostic. The tulip is a beautiful flower marvellously cultivated in the Netherlands, and since there are many Calvinists in the Netherlands and many flower-loving people, it seems to be a delightful arrangement to organize these doctrines in terms of the letters of this word. However, I would like to consider the nature of the points and suggest certain rewordings which, in my judgment, may prevent misunderstandings.

Radical and pervasive evil

The first point is 'total depravity'. The purpose of this point is to emphasize that no expectation can be entertained from man with respect to ability to please God or even to come to him in salvation unless God moves him to it. Thus, the purpose is further to turn away the eyes from man in his action and

47

ability and instead direct the eyes to God and his sovereign action. The advantage of expressing this truth in that way is that we emphasize the fundamental and pervasive character of the evil in man.

The terms that are used are somewhat misleading, however. I find that invariably, after having said 'total depravity', the staunchest Calvinists find it important to qualify precisely what they mean. They add, 'But we don't mean to say by this that man is quite as bad as he could be.' Practically everybody who says 'total depravity' or 'total inability' has to qualify this at once. Obviously, people who seek to know what Calvinism is ought to make it their business, not only to go by certain titles, but also to examine what is being said under those titles. But since those words are used repeatedly we cannot blame them too much for having taken them at face value. Nor can we blame them when, thinking that somehow Calvinists believe that every man is as evil as he can be, and finding situations where men seem praiseworthy, these people point to certain virtues and say, 'How can you hold to your Calvinism in the presence of this?' It would be wiser to use another form of language that would be calculated to emphasize the indispensable character of this divine grace and that would not need so quickly to have a qualification.

May I suggest that what the Calvinist wishes to say when he speaks of total depravity is that evil is at the very heart and root of man. It is at the very foundation, at the deepest level of human life. This evil does not corrupt merely one or two or certain particular avenues of the life of man but is pervasive in that it spreads into all aspects of the life of man. It darkens his mind, corrupts his feelings, warps his will, moves his affections in wrong directions, blinds his conscience, burdens his subconscious, afflicts his body. There is hardly any way in which man is called upon to express himself in which, in some way, the damaging character of evil does not manifest itself. Evil is like a root cancer that extends in all directions within the organism to cause its dastardly effects.

How shall we express this? Well, I am not too happy about my substitutions, but I think I would like to suggest that the term be 'radical depravity' or 'pervasive depravity' or, if you want to have a somewhat longer approach, to say 'radical and pervasive depravity'. This is a little less sweeping than 'total' and, in that sense, a little closer to what we really want to assert.

Divine initiative

The second point is 'unconditional election'. The emphasis here is upon the fact that it is God who takes the initiative. There is no previous merit or condition in the creature, either present or foreseen, which determines the divine choice. This is the key to what is in view. The disadvantage to this formulation is twofold. In the first place, it is not sufficiently comprehensive, for it suggests that the only thing that God does is to elect people to be saved and that, therefore, there is no relationship of God to those who are lost. But election involves not only the taking of some to be saved; it also involves the bypassing of the remainder of mankind and the just reprobation of them in view of their sins. So just to talk of election is not enough. We should also recognize 'preterition', the bypassing of those who are not to be saved. Moreover, the term 'unconditional' might be misconstrued to suggest that God has no interest in the condition of those whom he chooses to make his redeemed people. It suggests that God is not concerned about what we are, what we become, and how we relate ourselves to his will. If the point is that God does not ground his choice in the fact that those who are elected are better or worse than others, it is correct. But if it suggests that God does not care about the condition of those whom he has chosen to save, it is wholly incorrect. For the Scripture makes it very specific that we are elected 'unto good works, which God hath before ordained that we should walk in them' (Eph. 2:10).

What we need to recognize here is that the sovereign initiative in salvation is with God. It is not with man. It is not by virtue of something that God has foreseen in a man, some pre-existing condition which is the source or root of the elective purpose of God, that God saves him. God in his own sovereign wisdom chooses, for reasons that are sufficient unto himself, those who shall be saved. We may, therefore, much better speak of 'sovereign election and preterition'.

Particular redemption
Then comes the third point, which is sometimes called 'limited atonement'. This, I think, is a complete misnomer. The other points I can live with, but 'limited atonement' I cannot accept, for this is a total misrepresentation of what we mean to say.

The purpose of using this expression is to say that the atonement is not universal (in the sense of Christ having died for every member of the race in the same sense in which he died for those who will be redeemed). Therefore, the purpose of the atonement is restricted to the elect and is not spread to the universality of mankind.

Some limit it in breadth; that is, they say the Lord Jesus Christ died for the redeemed and that he sees to it that the redeemed are therefore saved. For them there is a certain group of mankind, a particular group, which is the special object of the redemptive love and substitutionary work of Jesus Christ and toward which Christ sees to it that his work is effective. While the remainder of mankind may gain some benefits from the work of Christ, they are, however, not encompassed in the same way in his design as were those whom the Father gave him. This is one way of limiting it. Other people say that Christ died for everybody in the same way, but they must acknowledge that some of the people for whom Christ died are at the end lost. So for these the death of Christ does not, in fact, insure the salvation of those for whom he died. The effect is to limit the atonement in depth. The atonement is ineffective. It does not secure the salvation of the people for whom it is intended. For these the will of God and the redemptive love of Jesus Christ are frustrated by the resistance and wicked will of men who resist him and do not accept his grace. For these, salvation really consists of the work of Christ, plus some ingredient of one kind or another that some people add like non-resistance. It is *this* ingredient which really constitutes the difference between being saved and being lost. No one who says that at the end there will be some people saved and other people lost can really in honesty speak of an unlimited atonement.

For these reasons I, for one, am not happy to go under the banner of a limited atonement, as though Calvinists and myself were ones who wickedly emasculate and mutilate the great scope and beauty of the love and redemption of Jesus Christ. For it is not really a question of limits. It is a question of purpose. How should we phrase it therefore? We ought rather to talk about 'definite atonement'. We ought to say that there was a definite purpose of Christ in offering himself. The substitution was not a blanket substitution. It was a substitution that was oriented specifically to the purpose for which he came into this world, namely, to save and redeem those whom the Father has given him. Another term that is appropriate, although perhaps it is less precise than 'definite atonement', is 'particular redemption'. For, the redemption of Christ is planned for particular people and accomplished what it purposed. The only alternative is that Christ redeemed no one in particular.

If we change the language in this way I think we avoid being the ones who seem to be in the business of restricting the scope of the love of Christ. If I say that my position is that of limited atonement, my opponent will say, 'You believe in limited atonement, but I believe in unlimited atonement.' He seems to be the one who exalts the grace of God. But see what happens when we use my words. I say, 'I believe in a definite atonement.' What can my opponent say? 'I believe in an indefinite atonement'? If I use the old language, I have no opportunity to do anything except protest. If I use the new language, I do not put myself at a psychological disadvantage from the start. Incidentally, the term 'definite atonement' you will find in writers such as John Owen the Puritan and William Cunningham of Scotland. So let us abandon the expression 'limited atonement', which disfigures the Calvinistic doctrine of grace in the work of Christ. The atonement is either effectual or universal. It cannot be both at the same time.

Effectual grace
The fourth point is 'irresistible grace'. The emphasis here is upon the fact that God accomplishes his designs, so that the saving grace of God cannot be resisted unto perdition. But a misunderstanding may also arise from this phrase; for it may suggest that a man may resist to the very end and that God will nevertheless press him willy-nilly, kicking and screaming, into the Kingdom. This is not the case. The grace of God does not function against our wills but is rather a grace which subdues the resistance of our wills. God the Holy Spirit is able to accomplish this.

You say, 'How can God the Holy Spirit accomplish this without violating free will and making us into puppets?' I don't know how he can do it, but that is what he does. I am not concerned about God's modes of operation, and I am quite ready to see that he may well have a good number that

I do not know about and that I am not able to explore. What I do know is that when there is resistance God comes in with his mighty grace and subdues that resistance. He makes no one come against his will, but he makes them willing to come. He does not do violence to the will of the creature, but he gently subdues and overcomes human resistance so that men will gladly respond to him and come in repentance and faith. We ought not to give the impression that somehow God forces himself upon his creatures so that the gospel is crammed down their throats, as it were. In the case of adults (those who have reached the age of accountability) it is always in keeping with the willingness of the individual that the response to grace comes forth. This is surely apparent in the case of the Apostle Paul, for whom God had perhaps made what might be called the maximum effort to bring him in. He resisted, but God overcame his resistance. The result is that Paul was brought willingly and happily into the fold of the grace of God.

What we mean here is not 'irresistible' – it gives the impression that man continues to resist – but 'effectual'. That is, the grace of God actually accomplishes what he intends it to accomplish.

Perseverance of God with the redeemed

The last point is called 'the perseverance of the saints', and the emphasis is upon the truth that those who have been won by the grace of God will not lose out but will be preserved by God's grace to ultimate salvation. It means that it is not possible for one who is truly regenerate so to fall out of the reach of divine grace as to lose salvation altogether and finally be lost.

The advantage of this formulation is that there is, indeed, a human activity in this process. The saints are active. They are not just passive. In a true sense they are called upon to persevere. But there is a devastating weakness in this formulation in that it suggests that the key to this perseverance is the activity of the saints. It suggests that they persevere because they are strong, that they are finally saved because they show that kind of stability and consistency which prevents them from turning back into their original wickedness. This is never the case. The key to perseverance is the preservation by God of his saints, that is, the stability of his purpose and the fixity of his design. What is to be in view here is not so much the perseverance of those who are saved, but the perseverance of God with the sinners whom he has gloriously transformed and whom he assists to the end. We ought to talk about 'God's perseverance with his saints'. That is the thing that we need to emphasize.

A new acrostic?
We now need to review our terms: 'radical and pervasive depravity', 'sovereign election and preterition', 'definite atonement', 'effectual grace', and 'the perseverance of God with his saints'. Those are the terms I suggested. Unfortunately, the terms do not provide acrostics in English, French, German, Latin, or any other language I know of. So we have lost our 'tulip', that beautiful mnemonic device to remember these five points in a simple manner. Well, I think it may be worthwhile to lose it, if those other terms mislead people as to what it is we actually hold. We certainly don't want to sell our birthright, which is the truth, for a mess of pottage, which is an acrostic. If that is what has to be done, let it be done.

On the other hand, I do not want to finish altogether on this note. So I would like to suggest to you that there is a way in which we ought to unite the five points; for in a very special sense we ought to recognize that the five points of Calvinism are, in reality, not five separate doctrines that we assert almost as disjointed elements, but rather an articulation of one point which is the grace of God. Total depravity we may call "indispensable grace." It is the truth that without God's grace we can do nothing because we are so evil. Election, called in Scripture the election of grace, may well be called 'differentiating grace' or 'sovereign grace'. Definite atonement is 'providing grace', for it refers to that grace by which God has established a basis for salvation. The fourth point is 'effectual' or 'efficacious grace'. Perseverance of the saints may be called 'indefectible grace', grace that will never fail us. In this way we can see how the points simply formulate what Scripture presents to us concerning God's grace.

If you want to, you can make an acrostic that will read 'gospel'. The *g* would be 'grace'; the *o*, total depravity, would be 'obligatory grace'; the *s* would be 'sovereign grace'; the *p*, corresponding to definite atonement, would be 'provision-making grace'; the *e* is 'effectual grace'; finally, the *l* would be 'lasting grace'. I do not like this as well as I like my other terms, so I present it with some diffidence. But if you are hung up on an acrostic, use it. At any rate, get something that has more meaning than "tulip."

Even better, let us go to the heart of the gospel and say, 'Calvinism is the gospel,' and then spell it out. This is what the Reformed position was all about, after all. *Sola gratia!* By grace alone! That is what we are talking about. The five points of Calvinism merely conjoin to this. Moreover, we do not even have to go to the Reformation, we can go directly to the Scripture.

Here is a text: Jonah 2:9. It reads, 'Salvation is of the Lord.' And, in the New Scofield Bible, which I will even venture to quote for once, there is a beautiful little note at that place which says, 'The theme of the Scripture.' That is exactly it. Salvation is of the Lord! That is the theme of the Scripture, and the five points of Calvinism.

Grace
Obligatory
Sovereign
Provision-making
Effectual
Lasting

5

Particular Redemption

Particular redemption has proved the most controversial of the five points of Calvinism. Here Reformed thinkers occupy a minority position. If you ask what Roman Catholics think, assuming that they are still in the main tradition of the church (which is not always clear now when people claim to be Roman Catholic), they will say that they believe in universal redemption. If you ask those of Greek Orthodox, Russian Orthodox or other Eastern fellowships, they will say that they believe in universal redemption. If you ask orthodox Lutherans or Arminians, they will say the same. In fact, I am afraid that if you ask quite a number of Presbyterian and Reformed people, even they will say they believe in universal redemption, though some of their confessions do not seem to give them much support. So those of us who believe in particular redemption appear to be something of a minority within a minority.

Different Christian groups can so emphasize their distinctives as to get them out of proportion. That is a danger from which Reformed believers are not immune. As Reformed people we gladly recognize our common ground with other believers. We emphasize that we do not have the corner on the work of Christ. We know that he has redeemed great multitudes who are not in the Reformed camp. (They are not Reformed as long as they are on earth, though when they get to heaven the Lord will take care of that in an appropriate way.)

Moreover, a doctrine of definite atonement or particular

redemption should not in any sense interfere with the propriety and necessity of addressing an appeal to every man, woman and child we can possibly reach in the name of Jesus Christ. Authentic Calvinism has always confessed particular redemption and at the same time insisted on the universal offer of the gospel.

Points of agreement

When we discuss the doctrine of particular redemption it is important to have in mind precisely what is at stake. For there are many people who do not understand what the subject entails, and as a result they have an entirely mistaken view as to what Reformed people hold on this topic. I would like from the very start to emphasize three areas which are not in dispute.

First, the question is not about *the value of the death of Christ.* There is no one I know of in mainline Calvinism who would be inclined in any sense to say there are limits to the value of Christ's death. It is freely granted that what Christ suffered is so immense, in fact so infinite, that it would be amply sufficient to atone for all the sins of all the people of all ages in the whole world and in a thousand worlds besides, if these existed. It is freely granted by all parties that the work of Christ is strictly infinite in its value.

Second, the issue is not *whether there are benefits which flow from the death of Christ to people who are not saved –* benefits, I say, short of salvation. On the contrary, the fact that Christ has come into this world has provided a certain outpouring of common grace. It has justified the long forbearance of God with mankind and therefore given perhaps a new impetus for this forbearance. There is a reprieve for mankind at large which is the result of the work of Jesus Christ. There is the possibility of calling people indiscriminately to the benefits of the gospel, to the joy of being sharers in the family of the Lord, and of having redemption and forgiveness of sins. Therefore, no one who holds to particular redemption desires in any way to say that what Jesus has done was exclusively for the elect. Rather, the work of Jesus Christ has universal significance and, indeed, a cosmic impact that goes beyond the interest merely of the human race. It concerns creation at large. These are truths which are freely confessed by those who hold to particular redemption.

Third, it is not an issue of *whether in fact all people will be saved.* It is granted by all evangelical people that in the final analysis there will be some people saved and others lost.

This is often disputed in our day. Universalists believe that in the end God will manage to save everybody. They do not believe in an eternal hell. That may sound very generous, but it is grounded in an insufficient perception of the gravity of sin. Besides, it does not help us to attempt to be generous beyond what the Scripture reveals. If the Scripture could be construed to reveal that all people will be saved, I could not be happier. That would be wonderful, and I would rejoice without any kind of embarrassment. But it simply does not appear possible to view the Scripture in that light. God has made it very plain that there is to be a last judgment in which some people will be saved and others lost. In recognizing this, evangelicals of whatever theological persuasion agree that in the end there will be some people lost and therefore that the work of Christ does not actually effect the salvation of the whole human race.

The real issue

The question is really the *design* of the Atonement. The intention of God the Father in sending the Son and the intention of the Son in offering himself as a substitute are the issue. For whom did Christ die? Who were the people whom he had on his mind and in his heart as he was offering himself as a substitute for the new humanity? Was it the totality of mankind, the saved as well as those who remain unsaved? Or was it those who, in fact, will be redeemed and may be seen as those encompassed in the elective purpose of God? As I indicated to you at the start, when that question is raised, the majority of Christendom answers, 'It is the former.' But those of Reformed persuasion say, 'It is the latter.' They say that our Lord died for the elect in a manner which is not shared by those who in the end will fail to receive salvation and will be lost forever.

At this point let me remind you that the language of 'limited atonement' is undesirable and unnecessary. It describes inadequately and unfairly the view held by Reformed people. The problem is that it seems to place the emphasis upon limits. It seems to take away from the beauty, glory and fullness of the work of Christ. We seem to be saying that is does not go quite so far as it should or could go.

The big question is not the question of limits. Everybody who does not hold to universal salvation has to grant that there are limits. Obviously if the limit is not in breadth, then the limit is in depth. If Christ offered himself for all men and all men are not saved, then obviously the *effectiveness* of the work of Christ is not without limits. It fails to accomplish what Christ intended to do. On the other hand, one could say that the work of Christ is intended only for those people who are saved. Here there is no limit to effectiveness, but there is a limit in the *intention*. And it is precisely this that the Calvinists are saying. The work of Christ was definite in its extent and wholly effective so that all for whom it was intended are going to be brought unto the ultimate enjoyment of salvation by the effectual power of God who works all things as he pleases.

The Reformed author Lorraine Boettner has compared the

matter to two bridges, one of which is relatively narrow but goes right across the river. The other is very broad but goes only halfway. It does not help very much. We have a bridge like that in France, the bridge of Avignon, but the only thing it is good for is dancing! In the matter of salvation we need a bridge that goes all the way from our misery in sin to the great blessings that God has provided for us.

Therefore, what we need to say is that the atonement is definite, that it is related to a particular people whom God has chosen. It is not a good idea to speak of a 'limited atonement'. I much prefer 'definite atonement' or 'particular redemption', and I would encourage other people to adopt these terms also.

Three arguments

I focus now on just three arguments out of many for the doctrine of definite atonement. If you want full argumentation for it, I cannot recommend anything better than *The Death of Death in the Death of Christ* by John Owen. And since that is a very complex work, I would encourage you to try to get a copy of the 'Analytic Outline' of it prepared by J. I. Packer.[1]

The *first argument* is drawn from the language that the Scripture uses to describe the work of Christ. One of the terms is 'redemption.' Redemption is that gracious and wonderful transaction by which our Lord Jesus Christ has purchased us to himself in order to liberate us from the slavery of evil under which we were held in bondage. If we take redemption seriously, we have to ask: What kind of redemption is this where some of the people who have been redeemed are still in bondage?

Suppose that for some reason a friend of mine has fallen afoul of the law and as a result has been taken to jail. I hear about his plight and immediately make my funds available to bail him out. In a very real sense I provide the price of redemption for him. All right. I get the bail, reach the prison, pay the money, and then go home. My wife asks, 'Where is your friend?'

I say, 'He's in prison.'

'In prison? But didn't you take the bail money down there?'

'Yes, I paid the money to redeem him, but he's still in prison.

It hasn't worked.' What kind of redemption would that be? If redemption is accomplished, then those who are in bondage must be liberated. They cannot be held in captivity any longer. Therefore, the work of Christ is described in such terms that not only what he intends but also what he performed is expressed by it.

Take the word 'propitiation.' Propitiation describes how by virtue of the death of our Lord Jesus Christ the wrath of God against us as sinners is assuaged. Therefore, God deals with us not in terms of his just wrath against sin but in terms of his fatherly and gracious concern as one who has received us into his household. What kind of propitiation would this be where those who are the beneficiaries of it are still under the wrath of God? That is what universal atonement would suggest – that there are people for whom Christ made propitiation who nevertheless are still under the divine wrath so badly that they will have to endure eternity in hell. The very nature of propitiation demands that the wrath of God should be taken care of for those who are the beneficiaries of it.

The work of Christ is also described as 'reconciliation.' What kind of reconciliation is it where the parties are still at enmity? Reconciliation like that is 'for the birds'! But that is the representation that is sometimes made about the work of Christ. The parties are still at odds. God is still angry, and the sinner is still God's enemy.

The very language of the Bible shows the work of Christ

to be not simply something that was intended and may or may not be effected, but rather the actual achievement of salvation. Redemption is accomplished. Propitiation is accomplished. Reconciliation is accomplished. This, I think, is plain. Therefore, a right understanding of the nature of the work of Christ drives us to definite atonement.

The *second argument* is even stronger. It is drawn from the nature of substitution. Here again, happily, evangelicals are at one to say, 'The work of Jesus Christ is a work of penal substitution. In dying on the cross of Calvary the Lord Jesus Christ as the substitute and representative for lost sinners bore in their place the full burden of their eternal condemnation for all their sin.' If we really accept this definition and do not try to fudge on it after we have first made our commitment, then the question must arise: What will there be left to condemn in the last judgment if Christ died in that sense for all members of the human race? What kind of condemnation will be left? The answer would have to be, None. Therefore, all should be saved. But it is quite plain that all will not be saved. So obviously Christ died as a substitute to bear the punishment due only unto the sins of those people who will not be punished.

God cannot punish a sin twice. He cannot punish it once in the person of the Redeemer and then punish it later in the person of the perpetrator. If it was punished in the person of Christ, then it will not be punished in the person of the sinner. If it is punished in the person of the sinner, then it was not punished in the person of Christ. The work of Christ is precisely related to the sum total of all the sins of all the elect in the whole world, and nobody else.

No one has put the matter more plainly than John Owen. Owen said, 'God imposed his wrath due unto, and Christ underwent the pains of hell for,

either all the sins of all men,
or all the sins of some men,
or some sins of all men.

If the last, some sins of all men, then have all men some sins to answer for, and so shall no man be saved.' That is obviously false; so option three is eliminated. The second case is: all the sins of some men. 'If the second,' said Owen, 'that is it which we affirm, that Christ in their stead and room suffered for all the sins of all the elect in the world.'[2]

But how about option number one, all the sins of all men? That is what the universal redemptionists say. 'If the first,' says Owen, 'why then are not all free from the punishment of all their sins?' You will say, 'Because of their unbelief; they will not believe.' But this unbelief, is it a sin, or not? If not, why should they be punished for it? If it be, then Christ underwent the punishment due to it, or not. If so, then why must that hinder them more than their other sins for which he died from partaking of the fruit of his death? If he did not, then did he not die for all their sins? Let them choose which part they will.'[3]

The truth of substitution must lead us irresistibly either to universal salvation or to definite atonement. Universal salvation is unbiblical and untrue and is a terrible snare to the church because it undermines its missionary endeavour. No universalistic church has ever lasted long. The only other alternative, the right one, is definite atonement. The intermediate view, universal redemption with limited salvation, really falls of its own weight in the presence of substitution.

My *third argument* is drawn from the nature of the Trinity and the unity of purpose between the Father, Son and Holy Spirit. According to those who hold to universal redemption, the Father would have chosen only some (on the basis of having foreseen their faith) and then have predestinated them to become like his Son.

This election terminates on only a portion of mankind. But then the Son would come and say, 'That's well and good, Father. But I am more generous than you. I am not satisfied to die only for these. I am going to die for everybody.' And then the Holy Spirit would say, 'The Father wins, because I'm not going to give faith and repentance to anyone except the elect. It's two to one.'

I do not wish to caricature the position of those who do not agree with me. But you have to realize that holding to universal atonement does terrible damage to the unity of the counsel of God. It is to separate the Father and the Holy Spirit from the Son, when the very essence of God is that there is one purpose in which they are united. What do we hear the Son pray? He says, 'Father, I want those you have given me to be with me' (John 17:24) – not everybody, but the people you have chosen. There is never a vacillation in this matter. It is perfect unity all the way through.

The problem texts
But there are people who say, 'The Scripture says otherwise.' And obviously if the Scripture says otherwise, then we will have to revise all our reasoning. Because in the end it is the Scripture that must decide, not the logic, rationality or conclusions that we draw on the basis of some scriptures. But does it say otherwise? There are three types of passages which are alleged to do so. First, there is a group of passages which are pressed into service to prove that *God has a universal saving will*. Passages of that type are found in Ezekiel 18:23, where God says, 'I have no pleasure in the death of anyone....so turn, and live' (RSV). Or 1 Timothy 2:4, where we read that God 'wants all men to be saved and come to a knowledge of the truth' (NIV). Or 2 Peter 3:9 which reads,

'The Lord is....not wanting anyone to perish, but everyone to come to repentance' (NIV). These passages are advanced to show that the saving will of God extends to mankind at large.

However, the passages in 1 Timothy and 2 Peter are not properly to the point. 2 Peter is emphasizing that God is not slack toward us, 'not willing that any [of the elect] should perish,' meaning that the Lord is not whimsically postponing his second coming; rather there is a purpose behind his delay. He wants to bring all the elect to repentance so that the whole people of God may be gathered in. 'The Lord is patient with you,' says Peter (not toward mankind in general but toward you Christians) 'not wanting anyone to perish,' but determined that all those marked for repentance should come to repentance.

The passage in 1 Timothy is best understood as Augustine and Calvin understood it, namely, that God is willing to save people from all categories of men. It is not only from some groups that he recruits his church, but God wills all kinds of men to be saved – even kings, unlikely as it may seem to be. Paul says, 'Let's pray even for them, even though you have very little expectation that they might come to salvation.'

Ezekiel gives expression to the merciful grace of God, who, strange as it may seem, does not find supreme joy in taking vengeance. Instead of that, we are told, God finds his supreme joy in the salvation of people. There is joy in heaven not only among the angels but even in the Father's heart when a sinner repents. That does not mean, however, that he has therefore designed to save all mankind.

The second group of passages are those in which it is suggested that *some people for whom Christ died may or will perish*: Romans 14:15; 1 Corinthians 8:11; Hebrews 10:27 and 2 Peter 2:1.

In the case of those who might seem to perish (Rom. 14:15; 1 Cor. 8:11), Paul makes it plain that they will, in fact, not perish (Rom. 14:4). But he castigates the carelessness of some Christians who are so totally oblivious of the spiritual concerns and needs of their fellows that they utterly disregard their interests and welfare. For the sake merely of some kind of food they will surrender to temptation some for whom Christ showed such great concern that he died for them.

Hebrews 10:27 and 2 Peter 2:1 show that the people involved had made strong professions of being members of the body of Jesus Christ. They had joined the church, shared in the sacraments and claimed that they were part of the redeemed people of God. Yet after having made all these professions, in due course they turned away altogether. They began to teach evil doctrines and even reviled the people of God. They turned persecutors. In this case, both the author of Hebrews and Peter say that these will be lost. It would seem to me that the wisest way of looking at these passages would be to regard the apostle as describing these persons in terms of what they claim, rather than in terms of what they had. In any case, the verses also present difficulties in regard to the doctrine of perseverance if they do not refer to profession only.

The whole world?

The most important group of passages are those in which *the work of Christ seems to be oriented toward the whole world.* Various terms are used. We have passages like 1 Timothy 2:6, in which we are told that Jesus Christ 'gave himself as a ransom for *all men.*' Romans 5:18 says that 'as through the trespass of one, judgment came unto all men, so through the righteousness of Christ justification came to *"all men".*' Second Corinthians 5:14-15 reads, 'One died *for all,* and therefore all died. And he died *for all* that those who live should no longer live for themselves, but for him who died for them and was raised again.' Romans 8:32 says, 'He who did not spare his own Son, but gave him up *for us all* – how shall he not also, along with him, graciously give us all things?' We have Isaiah 53:6, which says, 'All we, like sheep, have gone astray….and the Lord has laid on him the iniquity of *us all*.' Hebrews 2:9 declares that Jesus 'tasted death for *everyone*.' John 1:29 observes that Jesus is the Lamb of God that takes away 'the sin of *the world*.' John 3:16 says that 'God so loved *the world* that he gave his one and only Son.' In John 4:42 we read that he is 'the Saviour of *the world*.' John 12:47 says, 'I did not come to judge *the world*; but to save it.' 2 Corinthians 5:18, 19 says that God was in Christ, 'reconciling *the world* to himself.' We read in 1 John 2:2: 'He is the [propitiation] for our sins, and not only for ours but also for the sins of *the whole world*.' These are only representative passages, but I trust I have not omitted any that are considered immensely significant by those who advocate universal redemption.

This complex of passages is thought to create a tremendous presumption that our Lord in fact accomplished his work for humanity at large. It is thought that definite atonement is ruled out by these universal expressions.

When this kind of presentation is made it behooves us to observe the context rather carefully. This is particularly important with the word 'all', for 'all' may differ in its scope. If I say, 'I hope that all will retain their Philadelphia Conference on Reformed Theology badges,' you understand what I mean. I mean all delegates. I do not mean all men, women and children in the world. Sometimes when I have a class I describe the requirements for the course and say, 'All will turn in a term paper on such and such a day.' If that were to mean every man, woman and child in the whole world, I would be crushed under the burden of term papers that would be turned in. Obviously, the 'all' is related to the class I am teaching.

That is exactly what we have in many of the passages I have just quoted. Take Isaiah 53 as one example. It says, 'The Lord has laid on him the iniquity of us all.' But the ones in view are the ones who attain unto peace: 'the punishment that brought us peace was upon him' (v. 5). They are not people who continue to be at war but people who are now at peace with God. They are people who have been healed – 'by his wounds we are healed' (v. 5) – not people who continue to be sick in a spiritual sense. In that same context the prophet talks about 'the transgression of my people' (v. 8), not the transgression of all mankind. 'He bore the sin of many' (v. 12), not all. The people whose iniquities are borne are the same as those who are justified (v. 11), therefore, they are the redeemed. To assume that Isaiah 53 teaches an indiscriminate, universal redemption is to go counter to the very statements found in the chapter.

Take Romans 8:32: 'He who did not spare his own Son, but gave him up for us all – how will he not also, along with him, graciously give us all things?' How could anyone possibly imagine that this passage refers to the totality of mankind? The Apostle has just spoken of the elective purpose of God, culminating in the calling, justification and glorification of his people (vv. 29,30). Immediately after this he says, 'Who shall bring any charge against those whom God has chosen?' (v. 33). The idea of election is right there in the text. Again, he says that God has given us 'all things'. What is the use of receiving all things if you are in hell? Obviously, the people in question are the redeemed, people who will not be accused by God or separated from the love of Jesus Christ (vv. 38,39).

Second Corinthians 5:15 is immediately applied to Christians: 'He died for all that they who live should no longer live for themselves, but for him who died for them and rose again.'

The most difficult passage is 1 John 2:2: 'not only ours [our sins], but also for the sins of the whole world.' It is difficult because John seems to be making a contrast between an atonement restricted to Christians and one that extends to mankind at large.

When we consider that passage we have to give close attention to the fact that the term 'propitiation' is found there. This is a strong term that describes not only an intention but an effect. Here the Father is appeased. Christ is the propitiation, and therefore the wrath of God is assuaged. If 'the whole world' really means the totality of mankind, the passage will be proof of universal salvation and not merely of universal atonement. But does the passage prove universal redemption at all? Those who suggest that it does, say so. They suppose it to teach that Christ is the propitiation for the sins of us Christians, and not only for the sins of us Christians, who are in fact saved, but also for the sins of all other people, who are not saved. On the face of it, one could accept this interpretation – if this were the only passage we had, but we are not limited to this one interpretation. Several others are possible.

First, John may be emphasizing the exclusiveness of the work of Christ as the means of salvation. What he says would therefore refute the view that 'Christ died for our sins, and not only for the sins of us Christians who would receive propitiation by the work of Christ, while other people might have other means whereby God is propitiated toward men! No, 'Christ is the propitiation for the sins of all the people in the whole world who will experience propitiation. There is no propitiation outside of him.' This would tie in with what he says a little bit later in that same epistle: 'He who has the Son has life; he who does not have the Son of God does not have life' (5:12).

Another suggestion is that the apostle was emphasizing

that the work of Christ was not restricted to a narrowly conceived group, the Jews, but rather that the purpose of God encompassed much more than the Jewish race. The earliest Christians were all Jews; it seemed almost inconceivable to them that God would go outside the boundaries of the Jewish nation to shower his blessings upon mankind. They thought that the Jews were the primary and perhaps exclusive channel of divine blessing. The apostle John may have meant, therefore: 'He is the propitiation for our sins, and not only for the sins of us Jewish people – Christians of Jewish extraction or some other narrowly conceived group – but he is the propitiation for the sins of people who are recruited from all kinds of categories throughout the whole world, people of every tongue, language, race and nation under heaven.'

There is a possibility that the apostle wanted to emphasize the timeless character of the work of Christ: 'He is the propitiation not only for us who live in this present age, while people in other ages might have to go to God in some other way; but he is the propitiation offered once for all the sins of all the redeemed from the time of the fall of Adam to the very end of the world.'

These views are not in conflict. It is possible that the apostle may have meant to suggest all of them, and certainly when we read this passage we are not shut off to only one interpretation.[3]

Jewel of God's grace

In the Old Testament there is a great passage in which the high priest of Israel was told to wear upon his heart a breastplate in which the names of the tribes were to be inscribed (Ex. 28:29). As he entered into the presence of God, he was therefore bearing into God's presence the names of those whom God had been pleased to call in his mercy. This is a foreshadowing of the work of Jesus Christ, our great high priest, who came not with an indefinite, indiscriminate intent, but who came with the precise intent of being the redeemer of his people. These names are on his heart. These people are in his prayers (John 17:9, 20; Rom. 8:34).

You ask, 'Is my name there?'

I answer, 'Believe on the Lord Jesus Christ, and you will never find that your name is not there.' Repent and believe. Accept the grace which Christ offers to you, and do not fear that you will ever hear Jesus declare, 'Sorry, there is nothing here for you; your name is not on the list.' The very people who repent and believe, by that act prove that they *are* on the list. They prove that they are the beneficiaries of the work of Christ. Their faith, repentance, perseverance and commitment is a fruit of God's Spirit, secured for them by the work of the Saviour.

May no one ever think that definite atonement prevents anybody from coming, harms anyone or takes from anybody anything that belongs to him or her. On the contrary, definite atonement is a doctrine which shows a finished, accomplished salvation. This is not some mere potential which awaits its fulfilment from the accomplishment of some unrealizable condition. This is something concrete, effective, that has been wrought and which God himself in his mercy offers to us. May the Lord grant us the assurance that the Saviour loves us by name. He gave himself for the church (Eph. 5:25). His love is a discriminating and exclusive love. Therefore, let us not hesitate to proclaim the truth of particular redemption and rejoice in it. It is the heart of the great jewel of the truth of sovereign grace.

Notes

1. This outline is found in *The Death of Death*, Banner of Truth Trust, 1959, pp. 26-31.

2. *The Death of Death*, Banner of Truth Trust, 1959, pp. 61-62, or again, John Owen, Works, Vol. 10, Banner of Truth Trust, 1967, pp. 173-74.

3. The objection that definite atonement invalidates the sincerity of a universal offer is discussed in chapter 10, pp.

6

The Doctrines of Grace in the Teachings of Jesus

We have clarified the five points of Calvinism as 'radical and pervasive depravity', 'sovereign election and preterition', 'definite atonement', 'effectual grace' and 'the perseverance of God with his saints'. We have brought forward scriptural proofs for these doctrines. But an important question remains: Does Calvinism find support in the teachings of our Lord Jesus Christ? Or, to put it differently, are there statements that Christ made which give evidence of the doctrines of sovereign grace, those doctrines which have been the centre of Reformed thought?

When we raise the question 'Is there support in the teachings of our Lord for the tenets of Calvinism, for the doctrines of sovereign grace?' we do not suggest that if by any chance there were no support these tenets would therefore be false. Our Lord did not indicate that he taught us everything, as though the whole substance of Christian doctrine should be found in his words rather than in Scripture as a whole. We recognize that the whole Bible is to be the norm of our faith, not merely one portion of it which may be found in red in our red-letter New Testaments. At the same time, however, it is also true that the statements of our Lord are especially dear to our hearts. So obviously what he thought important to present to his apostles and to convey through their pen is of paramount significance among those who are Christians.

Furthermore, in some cases these teachings might find acceptance in places where other portions of Scripture might be rejected. In some quarters of Christendom we find some people who say, 'I do not care what Paul said; show me what Jesus taught.' Or some people may be so bold as to say, 'Paul erred on this thing.' Or again, 'Paul was a male chauvinist, but I want to stick with the statements of the Lord Jesus Christ.' So while we would be quite ready to recognize that in God's own providence the whole of the Bible is normative for us, it remains that sometimes it is valuable to check precisely what Jesus himself taught and attempt to synthesize his message.

You may wonder whether there is very much that Jesus said that relates to the doctrines of sovereign grace, and I suppose that I am going to stun you here with a little bit of statistics. In connection with this special occasion I will not hide from you that I went to the New Testament (the New Testament with red letters which is generally reliable as to what actually comes from the lips of our Lord) and made it a point to read again everything that Jesus said – all seventeen hundred and eighty verses of it. And I will confess to you that I was dumbfounded to find how very many passages actually relate to this topic. From the notes which I have, I judge that there are about five hundred passages that contain some reference to the doctrines of grace – almost one-third of what our Lord said. These verses relate to the evil in man that calls for grace, to the sovereign rights of God, to his wonderful provision whereby the Lord has given himself for the redemption of sinners, to the power of the Holy Spirit to attract sinners, and to his power to safeguard them to the end so that they will finally rejoice forever in the fellowship of their Lord.

So this is not a meagre section of the teaching of Jesus. This is not an area where we have to cast our net again and again and find it coming back empty. Almost any place at all that you cast your net you will find some statements of our Lord about grace. You will find them in Matthew, Mark, and

Luke; and you will find them in great abundance in John. John perhaps better than anyone understood the Lord Jesus. His Gospel is veritably filled with statements of our Lord which magnify the grace of God.

An evil generation

One of these points, the point of radical evil, emphasizes especially the utter need in which man is bound and which calls for the grace of God. The grace of God has to be manifested because man is totally helpless, because he is unable to lift himself in any way toward heaven. This does not mean that he is fully as bad as he could possibly be. This does not mean that you cannot find some little good in some men here and there. But it means that in relationship to salvation man is dead, depraved, and lost.

Our Lord Jesus Christ, with all the concern and compassion and love which he showed to mankind, made some very vivid portrayals of man's condition. He did not mince words about the gravity of human sin. He talked of man as salt that has lost its savour. He talked of man as a corrupt tree which is bound to produce corrupt fruit. He talked of man as being evil: 'Ye, being evil, know how to give good things to your children.' On one occasion he lifted up his eyes toward heaven and talked about an 'evil and adulterous generation', or again, 'this wicked generation.' In a great passage dealing with what constitutes true impurity and true purity he made the startling statement that out of the heart proceed murders, adulteries, evil thoughts, and things of that kind. He spoke about Moses having to give special permissive commandments to men because of the hardness of their hearts. When the rich young ruler approached him saying 'Good Master,' Jesus said, 'There is none good but God.' In this, incidentally, he did not mean to deny that he himself was good but, rather, he wanted to rebuke the man for the glibness with which he was

using the term 'good'. The man was not ready to recognize
the one he addressed as God.[1]

Jesus compared men, even the leaders of his country, to
wicked servants in a vineyard. He exploded in condemnation
of the scribes and the Pharisees who were considered to be
among the best men, men who were in the upper ranges of
virtue and in the upper classes of society.[2]

The Lord Jesus made a fundamental statement about man's
depravity in John 3:6. 'That which is born of the flesh is
flesh.' So he saw in man an unwillingness to respond to grace:
'You will not come,' 'You have not the love of God,' 'You
receive me not,' 'You believe not.' Such sayings occur
repeatedly in the Gospel of John. 'The world's works are
evil,' 'None of you keeps the law,' 'You shall die in your
sins,' he says. 'You are from beneath, not of God. You are
not my sheep. He that hates me hates my Father.' This is the
way in which our Lord spoke to the leaders of the Jews. He
brought to the fore their utter inability to please God.[3]

Following another line of approach he showed also the
blindness of man; that is, his utter inability to know God and
understand him. Here again we have a whole series of
passages that we could read showing that no man knows the
Father but him to whom the Son has revealed him. He
compared men to blind leaders who are leading blind people.
He mentioned that Jerusalem itself did not know or understand
even the purpose of God and, as a result, disregarded the
things that concerned salvation. The Gospel of John records
him as saying that he that believed not was condemned already
because he had not believed on the Son of God. 'This is the
condemnation, that...men loved darkness rather than light,
because their deeds were evil.' He said that only the one who
has been reached by grace can walk not in darkness but have
the light of life. The Lord Jesus emphasized that it is essential
for man to be saved by a mighty act of God if he is to be

rescued from his condition of misery. Even in the Lord's Prayer the Lord teaches us to say 'Forgive us our debts.' And this is a prayer that we need to repeat again and again. He said, 'The sick arc the people who need a physician.' We are those sick people who need a physician to help us and to redeem us. He said that we are people who are burdened and heavy-laden. In him alone can we find rest. 'Except you be converted,' he said, 'you can in no wise enter into the kingdom of God.' He represents the situation of man as that of a creditor who had nothing by which he could absolve his debts. He tells us in the great parables of Luke 15 that our soul is like that of a child that is so estranged that he has forfeited any right to belong to the family of God.[4]

Here again in John the message comes with particular pungency: 'Except a man be born of water and of the Spirit, he cannot enter into the kingdom of God.' And once again – 'You must be born again.' There is a necessity here not only of some reformation or adjustment, not only some repainting of old walls, but a total renewal that is at the very roots of the personality. Therefore he says that the one who knows him has passed from death unto life. 'No man can come except the Father draw him.' 'Except ye eat the flesh of the Son of man ye have no life in yourself.' He compares the situation of man to those who are in slavery and bondage, and he says that only in himself can one find freedom. 'The truth shall make you free.' 'The Son shall make you free.' 'If the Son, therefore, shall make you free, ye shall be free indeed. Without me, you can do nothing.'[5]

The people who received the greatest acceptance with the Lord were people who had this sense of need and who therefore did not come to him with a sense of the sufficiency of their performance. The people he received were those who came brokenhearted and bruised with the sense of their inadequacy.

Surely this is the meaning of the great parable of the
Pharisee and the publican. Judging by external standards the
Pharisee was head and shoulders above the publican, this man
who had probably been dishonest in raising the taxes of others
instead of being simply dishonest in paying his own taxes.
The Pharisee perhaps had only that latter defect, but in coming
to God he was really not lifting his prayer higher than the
roof. He was praying within himself. On the other hand, the
publican said, 'Have mercy upon me, O Lord. I do not deserve
any consideration or any help. I am depraved, I am helpless.
I plead, have mercy on me.' And the Lord Jesus said that he
went to his home justified, rather than the other.[6]

This again is beautifully represented in the parable of the
Prodigal Son, who said, 'I am not worthy to be called thy
son.'[7]

God's power

Not only does the doctrine of grace tell us about the great
need of man. It also tells us about the great ability of God to
respond to this need. The Lord Jesus Christ has exalted the
sovereign power of God. He has represented God as capable
of doing anything he pleases. He has shown that he is the one
who exercises judgment over the whole world. He sustains
even the flights of little birds by his almighty power. He is
the one who appoints the destinies of individuals and of
nations. He is the one who is capable at one word of healing
somebody who may have been paralysed for a long time.
'All things,' says the Lord Jesus, 'are possible with God.'
With man it is impossible. It is impossible that a rich man,
for instance, should come into the kingdom; but with God all
things are possible.[8]

Therefore the Lord Jesus Christ encouraged his disciples
to look to God with confidence. He did not say, 'Watch out
that you do not ask God anything that is too difficult for him.

Just show a little restraint in your prayer and adjust your request to the powers and provisions that God has at his command.' No, sir! He does nothing of the kind! He says, 'The sky is the limit! Go right ahead and ask what you want, in my name, submitting your will to the will of God and trusting that God is able to move mountains to manifest his sovereign mastery of the universe.'

Even in his address to Pilate the Lord Jesus made that very plain. He said to Pilate, the powerful Roman governor, 'You would have no power over me if it had not been given to you from above.'[9]

Our Lord did not suggest that we are to introduce qualifications by saying, 'Well, God's power is limited by the ability of man to resist. The free will of man needs to be taken into consideration and may sharply curtail what God is able to accomplish.' *There are no limits* to what our Lord presented. Granting fully that our Lord recognized the reality of human agency, rationality, and freedom, he never presented these as introducing a restriction or a qualification upon the sovereign power of God. Thus we have not only sovereign power but sovereign decision as well. The decisions of God embrace the destinies of men. They are decisions that are granted in his good pleasure and which are not always proportioned to what you might call the ability of man to respond. For instance, the Lord Jesus shows that there are people who might very well have benefited by the ministry that he performed but who were not privileged to receive it. He says that Sodom and Gomorrah would have repented if they had been exposed to his ministry, but they did not get it. He says that Tyre and Sidon would have repented if they had been privileged to see the kind of miracles which Capernaum and Bethsaida saw, but they did not receive this vision.[10]

Why is it that God did not give to these people the blessing that he bestowed on others? No answer is forthcoming. Our

Lord does not feel that God owes accounts to us as to why he does one thing or another. Everything he does in the area of salvation is purely of grace. What we deserve at his hand is condemnation. So, rather than to say, 'How come, Lord, that you do not do for me as much as you do for somebody else?' we should come to him and say, 'How wonderful, O Lord, that in your mercy you have not allowed me to perish in my sin and rebellion, which amply deserved any condemnation that I would have received from you.'

This, I think, is the drastic error which our Pelagian friends are making. They speak as if man had a right to come into the presence of God and enter into account with him, as if God had some obligation to deal with all people alike. The one thing God owes us is judgment. The thing that ought to cause us to marvel is the fact that instead of confining us all to judgment and damnation, God has been pleased in his mercy to make plans to save a great multitude. He has caused these to hear the gospel, receive forgiveness in Jesus Christ, be drawn in faith and repentance by the Holy Spirit so that they respond to the offer of the gospel, and be preserved to the end so that they will spend eternity in the blessed presence and fellowship of God. This is the thing that is marvellous. The fact that this has not been done for the whole of the race does not provide us with the proper ground for recrimination.

This is plain from the attitude of our Lord. Remember that great parable of the workers of the vineyard, where Christ expresses precisely this principle. He makes the owner of the vineyard say, 'My friend, I do you no harm. Am I not free to do with my property what I please? And if I want to pay somebody who has worked only one hour as much as somebody else who has worked twelve hours, that is up to me, so long as I have not defrauded you in the salary that we had arranged together.' This parable causes some difficulty, but this is a parable of Jesus. This is the way in which our

Lord, it would seem, by parabolic teaching shows us that we have no proper ground to recriminate against God for what may appear to us at times to be his arbitrary decisions.[11]

God's perfection includes wisdom. So nothing that God does is without an appropriate ground. But we do not always have to know what this ground is. In this we should be like children. Once in a while children ought to obey without knowing for what reason the parents give a commandment; otherwise they do not really obey the commandment, they obey the reason. So do we need to be submitted to God's sovereign decisions.

The Lord Jesus speaks frequently of the elect. There are eight different passages. In John 15:16 he says, 'You have not chosen me, but I have chosen you, and ordained you, that ye should go and bring forth fruit, and that your fruit should remain.' Some say this is not election to salvation; rather it is an election to service. Perhaps. But there is more in the statement of our Lord than simply the question of who was called to service. In a true sense there is sovereign determination in the matter of who it is who can hear the Word of God, for the Lord said that no man can come except the Father draw him (John 6:44, 65).[12]

In all this our Lord never dismissed the reality of human freedom. That is explicit even in regard to the great passage that I just quoted – 'You have not chosen me, but I have chosen you.' The disciples would have said, 'This is literally true.' It was not they who had made application in triplicate to be included in the college of the Apostles, or answered fifty-five questions in five different copies in order to become citizens of the United States – as I had to do some time back. No, in every case Christ took the initiative. He saw Peter and Andrew fishing and said, 'Follow me, and I will make you fishers of men.' He saw Matthew at his tax table and said, 'Follow me.' Every one of the disciples came into that position by the direct initiative of Christ. But notice – this did not obliterate their will. None of those people was mandated by a policeman. None was dragged willy-nilly behind our Lord in his journeys. They came of their own will. They came willingly. In other words, he did not make them go against their will; he made them willing to go.[13]

So the reality of God's action does not pre-empt the reality of our free agency. The kind of Calvinism that dismisses the reality of freedom of agency is a truncated Calvinism. It is not true Calvinism because it is not truly biblical. We need to recognize that God does not deal with man as one deals with pieces of wood or iron, with inanimate matter, with puppets, or with anything of that kind; he deals with man in terms of the rational agency that he himself has created and which reflects in some respects the wonderful image of God.

Definite atonement

Not only does Christ talk about election to salvation but, in his dealings with Judas, he gives us some inkling of that dark and difficult doctrine of reprobation. He said that he had lost no one except 'the son of perdition', that the Scripture should be fulfilled (John 17:12). The Scripture is very sober on this. Never does it suggest for even one moment that the ground of reprobation is some arbitrary condemnation by God. The ground of reprobation is always the sin of man and yet, ultimately, there is a sense in which God has made the sovereign decision as to who will be elect and who will be reproved.

This is echoed in the words of our Lord. The Lord Jesus Christ emphasized that the atonement he was to offer is related in a special way to those who are redeemed. The Lord Jesus said that the Son of man came to give his life as a ransom for many, not for all. He repeated this in the institution of the Lord's Supper: 'This cup is the new covenant in my blood, shed for the remission of the sins of many.' In John he said, 'I have come that *my sheep* might have life. The good shepherd gives his life for *his sheep*.' And in the immediate context he makes the distinction between those who are his sheep and those who are not his sheep, so that the definite reference of the death of Christ is explicit.[14]

If that is not enough, note that our Lord expressly rejects the universal reference in at least one of his prayers, for he says, 'I pray not for the world, but for those whom you have given me' (John 17:9).

Now it is true that our Lord also recognizes some benevolence of God and of himself toward creation at large. He talks to us about the Father, who makes his sun to rise on the wicked as well as the good. He talks about the fact that it is not the will of the Father in heaven that one of the least of these little ones should perish. He says that God is kind, even to the unthankful. He says, 'Be ye merciful, as your Father in heaven is merciful.' He says, 'The bread that I shall give is my flesh, which gives life unto the world'; 'I give my flesh for the life of the world'; 'I will draw all men unto me.' He says, 'God so loved the world, that he gave his only begotten Son, that whosoever believeth in him should not perish, but have everlasting life.' So there is a sense in which there is a wide reference to the concern of God. Yet when the question is raised, 'For whom did our Lord design to give himself as a ransom and as a substitution?' the answer must be, 'For those who will, in fact, be saved and whose redemption has, in fact, been secured by the death of our Lord.'[15]

Effectual grace

The Lord Jesus spoke about the effectiveness of the grace of God: 'This is the work of God, that ye believe on him whom he has sent'; 'All that the Father gives me shall come to me'; 'Except the Father draw him no one comes unto me, and I will raise him up at the last day'; 'Every man that has heard me and has learned of the Father comes to me.' God has ways to make his grace effective. He can overcome the resistance of our wicked hearts and lead us willingly to repentance and faith so that we can embrace the grace that is offered to us.[16]

Lasting grace

In closing, the question may be: Does this grace, when it is once received, continue? Is it lasting, or can it vanish? Can our sins eclipse the benefits of the grace of God so that those who have once been redeemed may fall again into perdition, out of the range of divine blessing and back into the clutches of Satan?

Here again our Lord has most significant statements to make. He talks about the way in which the seed that is cast into good ground grows unto harvest. He talks about gathering the wheat into the barn and throwing away the tares. (The wheat represents the children of the Kingdom.) He talks about the fact that the gates of hell shall not prevail against the building of the Church of Jesus Christ. He tells us that Satan would deceive the elect if it were possible, but the implication clearly is that it is not possible. He speaks about giving everlasting life. And what kind of everlastingness is this which would end in this brief course of our pilgrimage? He says that he who believes in him shall never thirst. And how would that not be thirst if, in the end, in rejection of God we should consign ourselves once again to damnation? He says that this is the will of the Father that he should lose no one, but rather raise them up at the last day. He says that the Lord holds his sheep – that no one shall take them out of his hand; that they shall never perish, that he gives them eternal life. There is this accumulation of statements in John 10:28.[17]

What kind of a shepherd would this be who would say,

'All I care about is to be sure that the wolves do not come in and damage the flock. So I let the sheep wander as they wish. And when some of them get lost, I say to the owner, "Well, I can't help it; they got lost by themselves." ' In Switzerland we have quite a few shepherds, and one of the tasks of the shepherd is to be sure that the sheep (or the cows) do not get lost. If they do get lost, then there are accounts to be settled. The Lord Jesus is the Good Shepherd. He is not going to allow his sheep to wander away. That, in fact, is expressly stated. He gives them *eternal life*. They shall *never perish*. So it is not a good answer to say, 'Well, no one can snatch them out of his hand, but they sure can jump!' If they jump they will perish, and our Lord says the contrary.

However, there are warnings in our Lord's statements. He says that 'he who perseveres to the end shall be saved.' He says, 'Blessed is the servant whom the Lord shall find watching.' He gives us the parable of the Ten Virgins in which there are people who seem to be related to the wedding and who, in the end, do not have a share because somehow they fall asleep at the wrong time. He talks of others as unprofitable servants who, at the time of distribution, are cast out where there is weeping and gnashing of teeth. He gives us the example of Judas who, even though he was one of the Apostles, seemed to withdraw and actually to perish. He tells us in John 15 that every branch that does not bear fruit he takes away. So our Lord does not encourage us to take glibly and for granted the benefits of his grace. The doctrine of security is not one that is calculated to encourage a false security in people who are eager to do evil. It is a doctrine which is calculated to encourage the confidence of the child of God in the sufficiency of the care, watchfulness, and perseverance of God his heavenly Father.[18]

So every one of the great points of Calvinism finds direct support in the words of Jesus. Some of them find no better support anywhere else in Scripture. Did Jesus teach Calvinism? Was Jesus a Calvinist? Would the Author of all grace teach us concerning the doctrines of grace? Why, certainly! And it is our comfort and our refuge.

The one who taught us so eloquently on grace is the one who sits on the throne of grace to intercede for his own, to lift them up in the presence of the triune God so that God's blessing may rest upon them. Listen to these words of Jesus: first, John 6:44: 'No one can come to me, except the Father, who has sent me, draw him; and I will raise him up at the last day'; then again, John 10:27-30: 'My sheep hear my voice, and I know them, and they follow me. And I give unto them eternal life; and they shall never perish, neither shall any man pluck them out of my hand. My Father, who gave them to me, is greater than all, and no man is able to pluck them out of my Father's hand. I and my Father are one.' This is the doctrine of grace from the lips of Jesus Christ.

Notes

1. Matthew 5:13; 7:18, 19; 7:11; 12:39; 17:17; 16:4; 15:19; 19:8; 19:17.

2. Matthew 21:41; 23:3-36.

3. Luke 15:19, 21; John 5:40, 42, 43; 3:12, 18; 4:48; 5:38; 6:64; 8:24; 10:25, 26, 38; 16:9; 7:7, 19; 8:24, 23; 10:26; 15:23.

4. Matthew 11:27; 15:14; Luke 19:39; John 3:18, 19; 8:12; Matthew 6:12; 9:12; 11:28; 18:13; 18:25.

5. John 3:3, 5, 15, 16; 5:24; 6:24, 53; 8:34, 36, 32; 15:5.

6. Luke 16:9-14.

7. Luke 15: 19, 21.

8. Matthew 19:26; 25:31-46; 10:29; Luke 7:7.

9. Matthew 17:20; John 14:13, 14; 15:16; 16:23-26; 19:11.

10. Matthew 10:15; 11:21-24.

11. Matthew 20:13, 14.

12. Matthew 24:22, 24, 31; Luke 18:7; John 6:70; 13:18; 15:16, 19.

13. Matthew 4:19; 9:9.

14. Matthew 20:28; 26:28; John 10:11, 15.

15. Matthew 5:45; 18:14; Luke 6:36; John 6:33, 51; 12:32; 3:16.

16. John 6:29, 37, 44, 45.

17. Matthew 13:8, 23, 30, 43; 16:18; 24:24; John 5:24; 6:27; 10:28; 17:2; 4:14; 6:39.

18. Matthew 10:22; 24:13, 46; 25:10-13, 35; 26:24; John 15:6.

7

Reconciliation and Propitiation

Behind the five points of Calvinism stands the doctrine of the atonement. As we have looked into these points, we have been considering why an atonement was necessary and for whom exactly it was designed. Now, the term 'atonement' is found very seldom in the English New Testament. So it is rather surprising that the word is so common in theological language. Atonement, of course, is a genuine English word. It is made up of the preposition 'at', the numeral 'one' and the suffix 'ment'. It means the transaction by which people are brought 'at one'.

The word 'reconciliation', which is probably a more exact translation of the group of words for atonement, bears witness to the same kind of truth, for in reconciliation we have the transaction by which people who are estranged are brought back into unity and harmony. The prefix 're' suggests that there was an original condition of harmony which was disrupted; then there is a transaction that takes place which brings back unity to those who were estranged. We talk about friends who get into a quarrel of some kind or another and then are reconciled. They are brought back into an attitude of friendship. Sometimes we have this in a home where people who are married experience estrangement. This may even lead to divorce in which the marriage is cancelled before the law. But then there is reconciliation. The spouses are brought back into the conjugal relationship and hopefully redevelop a life of understanding and love.

Reconciled to God

The word 'reconciliation' is used in Scripture to describe our relationship to God. It is found in the New Testament in five places, in two of them in great concentration.

We find it in Romans 5, for example. 'Since we have now been justified by his blood, how much more shall we be saved from God's wrath through him! For if, when we were God's enemies, we were reconciled to him through the death of his Son, how much more, having been reconciled, shall we be saved through his life! Not only is this so, but we also rejoice in God through our Lord Jesus Christ, through whom we have now received reconciliation' (Rom. 5:9-11, NIV). In these verses the word 'reconciliation' or 'reconciled' comes three times. So obviously the Apostle was very concerned with this particular idea. When we have repetition of a word in Scripture it is clearly something that needs to be listened to, and this is the case here.

Then, in the other passage where again great concentration is found, 2 Corinthians 5:18-20, we read: 'God…reconciled us to himself through Christ and gave us the ministry of reconciliation: that God was reconciling the world to himself in Christ, not counting men's sins against them. And he has committed to us the message of reconciliation. We are therefore Christ's ambassadors, as though God were making his appeal through us. We implore you on Christ's behalf: Be reconciled to God.' Paul used the word five times in these three verses. So we have here a very strong scriptural emphasis upon the fact that there is enmity between God and men and that the work of Jesus Christ effects reconciliation. He brings back into a position of fellowship, blessing, love and trust those who were in some sense separated and estranged.

Man or God?

When we consider the language of Scripture we need to observe very carefully what this reconciliation entails. Here we find a number of people who emphasize that the reconciliation must be the reconciliation of men to God. That is, it is men who are enemies of God. It is their minds that are alienated. Therefore, they need to be changed. We sometimes hear the additional comment, 'God does not need to be changed because God is love and is always prepared to receive his children. The whole process needs to terminate on men. It designates a change of disposition on their part.'

Sometimes, in support of this approach, emphasis is placed on the parable of the prodigal son, where they say, 'Here the Lord Jesus Christ gives us the very essence of the gospel, and what do we find? Does the father need to have a change of attitude? Does the father need to have his wrath turned into compassion and love in order to receive his erring but repenting son?' The answer is obviously, No. The father is always ready to receive him. In fact, we can indulge the representation that he is at the window, watching to see if there is not a sign that the son is coming. He is watching the road, looking for his son to come back, eager to receive him. When he finally sees the son, he runs to meet him and press him to his heart. He does not say, 'You are all sweaty; go, take a bath, and afterward I'll give you a kiss.' No, he takes this wretched son who has dissipated his fortune in riotous living, and presses him to his heart, saying, 'Let us rejoice, for my son has come back.'

'All right,' some say. 'In this parable there is no place whatsoever for a change in the attitude of God, represented by the father. Therefore, people who insist on the wrath and justice of God and on the Atonement as satisfaction are really tarnishing the glory and beauty of the love of the Father for us.'

How shall we respond to this? The thesis I would like to commend to you is that while it is true that our enmity to God needs to be overcome and while it is true that we need to be changed radically – a change so great that only the term 'resurrection' can properly describe it – still the major emphasis of Scripture is not so much on the setting aside of our enmity to God, important as it is, but on the transaction through the work of Jesus Christ by which the demands of God are properly satisfied and a new attitude, involving a new outpouring of his blessing and fatherly concern and care, is made possible.

Moreover, lest we should be too much impressed by the argument from the parable of the prodigal son, we should note that the parable does not talk at all about Jesus. We have two people in the first part of the parable: the father and the disobedient son. So obviously our Lord did not mean to represent the whole gospel here. It was one aspect of the gospel only. The people whose view I attempted to portray have, I think, caught that aspect. But what they have not asked sufficiently is under what circumstances God can, without detriment to the interests of his justice, holiness and moral government of the world, receive sinners as if they were not sinners. It is precisely this that requires the work of reconciliation in its full biblical dimensions. Therefore, we cannot short-circuit the message of the gospel by omitting that ground on which the mercy of the father *can* be manifested without doing detriment to God's other attributes and purposes.

A first consideration showing that the reconciliation in view is first of all the reconciliation of God to us – that is, the setting aside of God's just grievances against us – can be developed in connection with those great passages cited earlier. In them the Apostle does not at all leave us in a quandary as to what he has in view. Romans 5:9 says, 'Since we have now been justified by his blood, how much more shall we be saved from God's wrath through him!' Here the wrath of God is presented as that from which we need to be saved. This is not a God who is indifferent to evil. This is not a God who tolerates evil by dismissing it lightly. It is a God who by virtue of his own righteous character must be burning with wrath against every iniquity.

Then again, we read that when we were God's enemies we were reconciled to him through the death of his Son and have received reconciliation (Rom. 5:11). These are not things that relate merely to some transformation within us but to something outside us secured by the completed action of Christ.

In 2 Corinthians 5, the matter may be even clearer, for in verse 19 we read, 'God was reconciling the world to himself in Christ' and then immediately, 'not counting men's sins against them.' The reconciliation that is spoken of is a process by which the sins of men which would naturally issue in condemnation are not counted against them. So the reconciliation in view is one by which God sets aside his own legitimate and necessary grievance against the sinner by virtue of the work of the Lord Jesus Christ who has assumed the burden of that sin. The Apostle makes patently clear that reconciliation involves God himself, reconciliation by which God through his own resourceful and sovereign action can graciously receive those who are sinners and not forfeit his rights as Judge of the world.

The wrath of God

This is made very plain for those who wish to read the Bible carefully, for the concept of the wrath of God is spread throughout Scripture. Leon Morris, who has examined this matter perhaps more carefully than anyone else in his great book *The Apostolic Preaching of the Cross,* has counted more than twenty different Hebrew words that are used to represent the indignation of God against evil. More than twenty words! I wonder if we could think of anything at all for which we would have more than twenty words in English. Yet the Old Testament has more than twenty different words for the one concept of the indignation of God against sin. Moreover, this outlook finds expression in more than 580 passages.

The wrath of God is not just an Old Testament idea either. It is found in at least a hundred New Testament passages too. Some of the most fearful are from the lips of Jesus himself, for no one spoke of the wrath of God as manifested in the harrowing of hell as strongly as Jesus did. The wrath of God is a persistent theme in Revelation, the very climax of the Bible, for that book has a tremendous outpouring of divine wrath – vials, seals and trumpets – almost all expressions of the judgment of God.

Here it is important to understand the T of Tulip. It is necessary to make a right assessment of the gravity of sin. Obviously, people who want to dismiss it as a mere *peccadillo,* a little thing that can be discarded readily, will not want to have a conception in which God is upset by evil. They will say, 'We are sinners, yes, but it really doesn't matter. It is of no consequence.' But that is not the biblical outlook on the matter. The biblical outlook is that sin is supremely displeasing to God. It was that way in connection with the terrible sin of David. God was exceedingly displeased (2 Sam. 11:27). So too is God exceedingly displeased with our sin, because it is an affront to him as the holy, sovereign One.

Many people who have a superficial view of the Atonement deserve the verdict of that well-known statement of Anselm, who, I think, epitomizes the matter in one pithy formula: 'You have not yet considered how grievous a thing sin is.'[1] It is only when we consider how grievous a thing sin is and how greatly displeased God is with it, that we are in a position to understand what it means to be reconciled to him and what was entailed in producing this reconciliation. Only then can we understand what great cost was necessary in order to bring those who have alienated themselves from God back to that position where again they may receive his great favour and blessing.

Propitiation and wrath

Here it is proper to emphasize the language of propitiation. 'Propitiation' is not a common word in our daily language. In fact, the people who translated the New International Version gathered that an average high school graduate would not understand it and so avoided it. I support them in this because I feel that the primary thing in translating the Scripture is to make plain what God has said. If we use words people have a hard time understanding, we are, I think, betraying our task. We need to find ways of expressing the matter plainly. That is what the New International Version has attempted to do. So the translators in passages which speak about propitiation here used the term 'sacrifice for sin.' This is not a full description of what is involved in propitiation, but it is a good attempt.

This term was used in pagan worship in reference to what might be called a process of celestial bribery. The ancients thought, 'The gods are irritated against me, so I have to make sure that I get them something that pleases them and will avert their wrath.' They were making some payments, as it were, bribes, in order to secure the gods' favour. This concept is so unworthy of the true God that one could easily think that the New Testament writers would shun such a word. They would say, 'That's a word we cannot use.' But in fact, so deeply were they convinced of the reality of the wrath of God that they did use 'propitiation.'

Of course, in the New Testament, propitiation is never a

process of celestial bribery. Propitiation is the gracious act of God by which he himself has made the provision that is necessary for the outpouring of his blessing, by which he himself has taken care that all the demands of the law and of justice be met, so the sinners might be received in grace. Propitiation involves recognition of the objective character of the demands of God; and the Scripture teaches that those demands are met by the work of Jesus Christ. The fact that the word 'propitiation' is used – once in Romans 3:25, twice in Hebrews and twice in 1 John – is an important evidence that the reconciliation the Scripture speaks about is primarily the reconciliation of God to man.

Two misrepresentations
Let us be sure, however, that the following two very unfortunate caricatures are not permitted to gain acceptance as a proper representation of the evangelical view. The first suggests that somehow the Father is the one who imposes the demands of justice, and thus he appears to us in the unlovable character of a judge, as an irascible, inflexible person who is going to have his pound of flesh. But Jesus is the one who is gracious and merciful and who comes forward and says, 'All right, I will offer what is necessary. You don't have to hold off in wrath and anger.' Then he offers himself for his people, according to this view, and the wrath of God is changed into love.

Obviously there is good reason to resent this kind of representation. It is not scriptural. It is not Reformed. I would like to warn people of Reformed thought never to make presentations that would give reason for people to construe the matter in this way. What we have here is the love of the triune God toward unworthy sinners by which the Father, Son and Holy Spirit together counsel to establish a plan by which these sinners may receive the blessings of divine grace rather than be exposed to righteous anger. In this process the Father draws the plan of salvation, the Son in full harmony with the Father effects that which is necessary for the setting aside of God's grievances against the sinner, and the Holy Spirit applies this blessing to the individual life so as to draw people effectually into the benefits of the divine grace. We never have the persons of the Trinity at loggerheads with one another. Wrath is not *changed* into love. Wrath is averted. Justice is satisfied. Demands are met. And as a result, the love and blessings of God are poured out upon those who believe on Jesus.

The second caricature comes from a failure to recognize the divine nature of the Son who has come as mediator. Notice that God did not delegate the task of bearing the weight of sin to a third party, but it is God himself (as Son) who paid the cost. The one who bears the full burden of divine wrath against sin is God, for 'God was reconciling the world to himself in Christ.' The marvel of the gospel is that God has been pleased to bear the burden of our penalty in full in order that we might be beneficiaries of the fullness of his redemptive grace.

Effectual reconciliation

How effective is this reconciliation? Is it truth or is it merely an illusion? Does the situation resemble certain ceasefires where the soldiers have presumably stopped fighting but there are still bullets flying back and forth? Not at all! Instead, Scripture represents the work of Jesus Christ as encompassing us in a covenant, a solemn commitment which God makes to us.

Hebrews says that Jesus is the mediator of a new covenant. 'By calling the covenant new he has made the first one obsolete' (Heb. 8:13). We read about being adopted into the family of God: 'Those who are led by the Spirit of God are sons of God' (Rom. 8:14) and 'By him we cry, Abba, Father' (v. 15). 'To all who receive him,' said John, 'to those who believed in his name, he gave the right to become children of God' (John 1:12). You remember the beautiful passage in 1 John where the apostle says, 'How great is the love the Father has lavished on us, that we should be called the children of God! And that is what we are! The reason the world does not know us is that it did not know him. Dear friends, now we are children of God, and what we will be has not yet been made known. But we know that when he appears, we shall be like him, for we shall see him as he is' (1 John 3:1, 2). 'If we are children, then we are heirs – heirs of God and co-heirs with Christ' (Rom. 8:17). 'The Holy Spirit...is a deposit guaranteeing our inheritance until the redemption of those who are God's possession – to the praise of his glory' (Eph. 1:13,14). Union with Christ is represented as the union of the plant with its branches (John 15), the head with the body (1 Cor. 12), the husband with the wife (Eph. 5).

The reconciliation that Christ has accomplished is one that sets aside God's grievances and introduces us by massive grace into the immensity of blessing that God has provided for us. The riches of the elect of God in Jesus Christ are described in Ephesians 1. That is what God has prepared. So let us accept and discharge with joy that ministry of reconciliation which God has given us: 'God was reconciling the world to himself in Christ' (2 Cor. 5:19).

Notes

1. Anselm, *Cur Deus Homo*, La Salle, Il: Open Court, 1962, p.228.

8

Justification: Standing by God's Grace

Atonement or reconciliation describes the heart of the gospel from God's standpoint. If we turn now to the human standpoint, to those who will benefit from this reconciliation, their primary blessing is that of justification. Justification is not a subject on which those who are distinctively Reformed, as compared with Lutherans, Arminians or perhaps even those of some other branch of Christendom, claim a peculiar corner. Since it is central to the gospel and a cornerstone of the whole Reformation movement, we can gladly express our full-fledged agreement with many of our evangelical brothers and sisters in other groups, emphasizing the exclusiveness of the work of Jesus Christ and its complete adequacy for those who trust him.

Let me start with a definition: 'Justification is that redemptive act of the triune God whereby, on the basis of the substitutionary work of Jesus Christ, the head and mediator of the new covenant, he declares the penitent and believing sinner to be free of all guilt and to be entitled to all the blessings secured by the perfect obedience of Christ.'

Acquittal in court

To help us understand justification the Scripture draws parallels from three major areas of life. These supplement each other by enabling us to grasp various aspects of this great blessing.

The first area is the law court. In fact, it is from this area that the word itself is drawn, for justification is a forensic term. It deals with the plight of someone who is exposed to the verdict of the tribunal. Justification specifically indicates that at the bar of the law court, where condemnation may well have been expected, there is acquittal. In the place of condemnation, there is a declaration that the prisoner has been found not guilty and has been cleared of the charge.

This particular emphasis of Scripture makes plain that we need to consider justification to be primarily the work of Jesus Christ *for us*, rather than the work of the Holy Spirit *in us*. Regeneration is the work of the Holy Spirit in us to renew our nature and call us to life. Justification involves, not our condition, but rather our *status* or *standing* before God.

This is made very plain by Scripture's use of the word 'justification.' For example, there is the Bible's statement of what is the opposite of justification. If what was in view was the condition of our nature, then the opposite of justification would be pollution, and justification would be seen as renewal. But that is not the way in which Scripture handles the matter. It shows that the opposite of justification is condemnation (e.g. Rom. 5:16,18). Consequently, justification means acquittal. It is the act whereby one authorized to make the pronouncement declares that the person brought to the bar is free of the charges against him or her.

Proverbs 17:15 may be quoted to prove that in Scripture 'to justify' means 'to declare righteous,' rather than 'to make righteous.' 'He who justifies the wicked and he who condemns the righteous, both of them alike are an abomination to the Lord' (NASB). If justification were a process whereby someone is restored to a right attitude or to a right character, we would have to say that one who justifies the sinner is pleasing to God. But justification is not a rehabilitation program. The sense of this text is that God does not countenance injustice. If people come to court, their case must be examined on its merits, not in terms of some preferential attitude the judge might have to one party or the other. In court he who declares the transgressor to be righteous, and he who condemns the innocent, both prostitute justice and are an abomination to the Lord. It is plain in this passage that justify means to declare righteous and nothing else.

We find another proof in Luke 7:29 which says that even the tax collectors 'justified God' (KJV). If 'to justify' meant 'to make righteous,' the tax collectors could not do this. God does not need to be made righteous. He is righteous in essence. He is the foundation of all righteousness. Nobody can in any possible sense make God righteous. What happened, however, is that these tax collectors were ready to acknowledge the rightness of God's claims expressed in the ministry of John the Baptist, while the leaders of the religious life of that time, the scribes and the Pharisees, in rejecting this ministry, were closing their eyes to the righteousness of God.

So, to justify is to declare righteous, and justification is the blessing by which God declares righteous those who are by nature not righteous.

It is important to see that in justification the principle of righteousness is present. For it is not as if God suddenly decided to wink at evil and say, 'I'm going to act as if this never happened.' On the contrary, in justification the justice of God is safeguarded. But how? God does not abdicate the office of moral ruler of the universe. God is not going to judge wrongly; he will not declare the guilty righteous and the righteous guilty. Yet, if we are to be saved at all, he has to do precisely this! How does he do it? He does it by placing our guilt upon the righteous Son of God, even Jesus Christ, and declaring us free of guilt by virtue of the work he has accomplished.

This might have been a travesty of the whole principle of justice. But because of the union that exists in God's mind between the mediator of the new covenant and those whom he represents, this is not a travesty but an exercise of justice. It is not a situation in which something that is iniquitous is accomplished in the name of the law. On the contrary, it is a place in which, through his infinite resources, God has manifested both love and wisdom in exercising his justice in full. In Christ he has punished in full the sins we have committed and has transferred Christ's blessings to us so that we, who are sinners, are acquitted in his court, and Christ, who is righteous, having voluntarily accepted this awful burden upon himself, is condemned. Christ absorbs to the full the awesome weight of the wrath of God, and he does it in order to secure freedom, acquittal and forgiveness for us. God does not dismiss evil. He does not cloud the principle of justice but rather brings it to its fullest and most emphatic expression.

It is very important that we should understand justification in the light of Calvary. God did not simply manifest his love at Calvary, although Christ's death is the supreme expression of divine love. But he manifested at the same time, and supremely, his justice, his righteousness. If we allow this factor to be moved out of the picture, the cross becomes a completely opaque enigma: there remains no point to the sufferings of Christ. Unless we have a substitution in which our Lord has taken the place of his own people before the bar of God, then the cross ceases to be effective in any other way.

Justification brings joy to the heart and soul of one who deeply senses his or her guilt. It provides a resolution of the problem of guilt, not a dismissal of it, not a glossing over it. Here there is no suggestion that we are somehow mistaken because we feel guilty. Some psychologists tell us: 'Don't feel guilty! Get rid of your guilt complex.' Well, there are some people who obviously are exaggerating guilt, and harm themselves in this way. But the basic problem with humanity is not that it has so much guilt but that it has so little. We tend to gloss over our misdeeds.

Justification comes not by something we have done, but by what Christ has done in our place. Our sin is not going to come forward as a huge charge against us. It has been expunged from our record because Christ died. He has borne to the full the burden of our sins; therefore, they are thrown behind God's back, as it were (Isa. 38:17). They will not count in the day of judgment. Luther gloriously perceived this truth and it led to the tremendous ministry that he was enabled to carry forward by the grace of God.

Forgive us our debts

A second line of illustration that the Bible uses to illustrate the blessing of justification is commercial. The Scripture describes us as being debtors, people who owe a rather large debt of money. We give expression to this in the Lord's Prayer when we say, 'Forgive us our debts, as we forgive our debtors' (Matt. 6:12).[1]

The imagery of debt is frequent in Scripture. There is a way in which we owe ourselves and our deeds to the Creator of our lives. We are not totally autonomous creatures, free to do exactly as we please. We are responsible agents who are answerable ultimately to the Almighty. On that account, to do something that is contrary to the will of God is like incurring a debt at the financial level. Here again, the Scripture makes plain that this is a burden that is simply unbearable. It represents the human predicament in terms that are staggering if we understand the text.

I call your attention to the parable that Jesus presented in Matthew 18:23-34. There he speaks about a servant who owed a debt to his master and, being unable to pay, was about to suffer for it. Everything he owned was going to be repossessed, and he and his family were going to be sold into slavery in order to contribute toward the payment of what he owed. He went to his master and pleaded for mercy. He asked for an extension of time. The master graciously cancelled his debt. Then this same man encountered somebody who had a small indebtedness to him: a hundred *denarii,* the payment for a hundred days of work. He took him by the throat and said, choking him, 'Pay what you owe me, or else I will invoke all the sanctions of the law against you.'

The point I want to emphasize is that our Lord called the first man's debt a debt of *ten thousand* talents. By the very fact that 'ten thousand' is there, you would imagine rightly that this is a fairly large sum. When we owe ten thousand of anything, it sounds bad. But the full impact of this is probably lost for us because we do not usually spend time figuring out how much a talent might be worth. A talent was a measure used for the weighing of precious metal, particularly silver or gold. Jesus did not specify whether these were ten thousand talents of silver or ten thousand talents of gold. But in view of what he means to teach, we can assume that these were talents of gold (although we have no way of proving it). The weight in question was approximately one hundred pounds. So the debt of this man would be ten thousand times one hundred pounds. That makes one million pounds, which would be the equivalent of five hundred tons of gold. Let us use as an average the figure of $300 an ounce. There are sixteen ounces in a pound. So a pound of gold is worth $5,000. One million pounds of gold are worth $5 billion! This man owed $5 billion! How could he ever hope to repay. We owe God a debt that is enormous! To earn one talent of gold would require at least fifteen years of normal labour. Ten thousand talents would mean 150,000 years of labour! How could anybody hope to pay that? So when Scripture talks about debts, it does not suggest, 'We'll disregard this; it is a small matter.' Scripture says, 'You have a crushing burden. There is no way by which you can meet the righteous demands of God upon you. You are undone! You are lost! You have nothing with which to pay! (Luke 7:42). The debt is staggering!' To appreciate the grace of God in justification we must be aware of the immensity of our debt. The term 'justification' embodies the truth that in Christ our debt has been paid; it is wiped out.

Scripture has repeated recourse to this commercial language, not because it wants to dignify business (although there is nothing wrong with business, provided it is honestly carried out), but to make us sense deeply that a transfer is involved. In judicial matters we do not have parallels in this respect. If somebody is a malefactor and I go to court and say, 'Release this man; I'm going to take his place,' the judge would say to me, 'Impossible! The law wants him, not you. This fellow is the one who is guilty, and I'm going to punish him.' The penal law does not permit substitutions. In the matter of debt, however, there is a parallel. If you are in arrears on your rent and come to me and say, 'You have money. Why don't you pay my rent for me?' I can go to the landlord and pay the money. If I do, you are free and the landlord has no way of saying, 'But I needed to get this money from that person.' It does not matter who makes the payment. Scripture uses commercial language because precisely at the commercial level the principle of substitution can so easily be illustrated.

Clothed in rich garments

Third, Scripture presents justification from the point of view of clothing. Our predicament here is that of being very miserably clothed. You may remember that great passage of Isaiah where he says, 'All our righteous acts are like filthy rags' (Isa. 64:6).

There are some people who are quite particular about how they clothe themselves, and there are others who do not seem to care. At seminary we have some people who seem almost to have made a virtue of being poorly attired. They seem to have no pride in the way in which they groom themselves, although I hope that by the time they candidate before a church they will have learned that there are situations where it is desirable to be at least decently arrayed. When you have a very special occasion, like a great public recognition, almost everybody senses that it is a time when one has to be properly and decently clothed. If we had a tremendous celebration designed to honour us or bring us into the public limelight, it would be a great humiliation for any of us to appear in tattered, filthy rags. But that is exactly what the Scripture represents us as doing. We are invited to a celebration of monumental proportion: the heavenly banquet in the presence of God himself, of God whose eyes are too pure to look upon evil (Hab. 1:13). And we are improperly clothed.

There is a parable of Jesus that deals with this also. A man had made a great banquet. He had provided garments for each of his guests. One person managed to get in without it. He was asked, 'How come you dared to enter with your own garment?' And then the master said, 'Throw this man out! He is an intruder and has no place in my celebration' (Matt. 22:1-14).

If we appear before God on the basis of our own performance, it will be an enormous discomfiture for us, a humiliation of all humiliations. In the most significant place, in the most signal and public manner, our shame and dishonour will be clearly exposed. Think for a moment what could happen to any one of us if suddenly, before everyone, there were inscribed on the wall in large letters all the sins that we have committed. We would want to melt out of sight rather than be thus exposed.

But now justification comes in, and justification involves two steps, as it were. First, the removal of these inadequate and filthy clothes. Then, the giving of a new garment which equips us for appearance with joy and confidence in the presence of God.

This particular line of thought is represented beautifully in the prophet Zechariah. Zechariah saw the high priest, Joshua, standing before God, and Satan there to accuse him. Satan would have been saying, 'You are not worthy! You cannot come into the presence of God! Look at all the evil things you have done!' Joshua was indeed arrayed in filthy clothes. But an angel of God was there and the angel said to those who were standing by, 'Take off his filthy clothes!' These symbolized his own performance, his failure. Then the angel said to Joshua, 'See, I have taken away your sin, and I will put rich garments on you.' Then he said, 'Put a clean turban on his head.' So they put a clean turban on Joshua's head and clothed him while the angel of the Lord stood by (Zech. 3:1-5). In this story, justification is represented as that blessing whereby God removes our own corrupt deeds and in place of them vests us with the immaculate and resplendent righteousness of Christ.

In these three forms of representation Scripture commends justification as a work of the immense grace of God which frees us from all fear of judgment, cancels out the frightful debt that we have incurred by our rebellion against God, and clothes us in a rich and glorious manner by virtue of our Lord's work. I repeat: Justification is that redemptive act of the triune God whereby, on the basis of the substitutionary work of Jesus Christ, head and mediator of the new covenant, he declares the penitent and believing sinner to be free of all guilt and to be entitled to all the blessings secured by the perfect obedience of Christ.

Special problems

I would like to add some brief comments in regard to special problems that arise. First, what is the relationship of justification to *grace*? I answer, justification is *by* grace. Justification is entirely gracious. It is not something earned. It is not deserved. It is something that God graciously gives to those who do not deserve it but whom he has chosen. The grace of God is the motivating source of justification.

What is the relationship of justification to *Christ and his work*? Christ has provided the ground for justification. It is entirely in the work of Christ that the basis for anything that God declares is to be found. It is what we sing so beautifully in the hymn 'Jesus, thy blood and righteousness my beauty are, my glorious dress.' That is what counts. It is the work of Christ that is the exclusive, meritorious ground of justification. There is nothing else. There is no performance, no contribution that we can make at this point. The work of Christ is the sole basis for this new way in which God deals with us.

What is the relationship of justification to *the work of the Holy Spirit*? Here we need to be very careful not to confuse the work of Christ *for us* and the work of the Holy Spirit *in us*. Regeneration is a part of the work of the Holy Spirit in us. It is the beginning, as it were. Justification is a blessing in which the Holy Spirit also has a share, but not by virtue of his work in us. Rather the Holy Spirit applies to each individually the benefits of the work of Christ. It is the Holy Spirit who implants us in Christ. It is the Holy Spirit who effects this union with Christ, outside of which there is no spiritual blessing. The Holy Spirit puts us into the category of the justified. However, the ground of justification is what Christ has done once for all, not something that the Holy Spirit is now doing (1 Cor. 6:11).

What is the relationship of justification to *faith*? Faith is the appropriating means by which justification can be obtained, secured and evidenced in our lives. We are justified through faith, because it is through that channel that we receive the blessing of God. Faith is not a meritorious action which would lead God to say, 'These believed; therefore, I am going to reward them and give them justification. Those others did not believe; so I am going to punish them for not believing; they will not get justification.' That is an error. Faith is not a work; it is a fruit of the gracious work of the Holy Spirit. Consequently, the ground of our justification is not faith but rather the work of Christ. Faith may be compared to an electric switch. The switch does not contribute one watt of power for the lights, but it must be switched on if the lamp is to light. We cannot say, 'It doesn't matter whether we believe or not,' for God has appointed, in the case of those who come to the age of accountability, that justification will be experienced and appropriated through faith.

What is the relationship of justification to *good works*? The ground of justification is not good works, not before we are justified, nor after we are justified. However, good works are mentioned in connection with justification, particularly in the Epistle of James.

Here I would not follow Luther and attempt to dismiss that epistle because it does not stress justification as the free blessing of God. James is doing something else. He is dealing with people who were wrongly claiming to be justified but who were showing that they did not have real faith by the fact that their faith was not operative. It was a dead faith. They were not acting upon the things they claimed to believe. So James tells these people, 'Don't ever think that you're going to get justification that way. The only faith by which justification is apprehended is a living faith. It is a real union with Christ.'

It is the same as grafting. If you put a twig in the general vicinity of a tree, it does not do anything. You must put it into the flowing stream of sap, otherwise there is no grafting. In the same way, James emphasizes that the faith by which justification is apprehended is a living faith that inevitably produces good works. Good works are an evidence of true faith. But they are not the ground of acceptance by God under any circumstances.

What is the relationship of justification to *rewards*? Justification deals with our basic relationship to God. It has nothing to do with rewards. Scripture also speaks of rewards, because God in his mercy not only is pleased to receive us in grace as his children, as those who have been forgiven and acquitted, but also to reward even that feeble measure of activity that we can muster for him. The rewards are an additional blessing, but they are not part of the justification itself.

What is the relationship of justification to *imputation*? Imputation is deeply connected with justification. Imputation is that reckoning whereby what ordinarily would be on the account of one person is transferred to the account of another. It is by imputation that our guilt has been placed on Jesus Christ so that he was enabled to bear the punishment due to us for our sins. It is by virtue of imputation that the righteousness of Christ is placed to our account so that we are seen not as naked but as clothed with the resplendent robe of Christ's righteousness. Imputation describes the methodology by which justification is accomplished.

What is the relationship of justification to *the resurrection of Christ*? It is said that 'he was delivered over to death for our sins and was raised to life for our justification' (Rom. 4:25). The sacrifice of Christ by itself is sufficient for freeing us from our guilt. But if Christ had not been raised, we would not know for sure that his offering achieved our justification. Therefore, the resurrection is the manifest proof that the sacrifice of Christ was acceptable, that the transaction has in fact been completed and that the freedom, deliverance and renewal of the people of God have been firmly anchored in Christ's work. The resurrection is a signal that justification is accomplished.

What is the relationship of justification to *time*? That is, when does God justify? Does he justify in his eternal purpose when he elects his saints? Does he justify when Christ died or when he rose from the dead? Does he justify when he moves by his regenerating power in the heart and life of an individual? Does he justify when we apprehend this truth and appropriate it by faith? Does he justify at the last judgment when he will declare us righteous by virtue of the righteousness of Jesus Christ? I answer, 'In some sense at least, all of these.' When the Bible speaks of justification, however, in the main what is in view is that appropriation of justification which takes place in time.

So here the great golden chain of Romans 8:28, 29 comes in: 'Those God foreknew he also predestined to be conformed to the likeness of his son [here is the eternal purpose]....And those he predestined, he also called [this relates to the personal experience of regeneration]; those he called, he also justified [again, this is something involved in our lives here and now]; those he justified, he also glorified [here we have the final link with eternity].' These five links do not represent all the elements that can be enumerated in the total redemptive purpose and acts of God. But there is still only this one chain, and it is constant. There is no vacillation, no shifting as to who is involved. Therefore, the blessing of justification, bestowed at one point, is joined to all the other blessings bestowed all along the line. I close with a quotation from Luther:

What man is there whose heart, hearing these things, will not rejoice to its very core and, in receiving such comfort, grow tender so as to love Christ, as he never could be made to love

by any laws or works? Who would have power to harm such a
heart or to make it afraid? If the knowledge of sin or the fear of
death break in upon it, it is ready to hope in the Lord; it does
not grow afraid when it hears tidings of evil, nor is it disturbed
when it shall look down upon its enemies. For it believes that
the righteousness of Christ is its own and that its sin is not its
own, but Christ's; and that all sin is swallowed up by the
righteousness of Christ as has been said above, a necessary
consequence of faith in Christ. So the heart learns to scoff at
death and sin and to say with the Apostle: 'Where, O death, is
thy victory? Where, O death, is thy sting? The sting of death is
sin and the strength of sin is the law. But thanks be to God,
which giveth us the victory through our Lord Jesus Christ.'
Death is swallowed up, not only in the victory of Christ, but
also by our victory, because through faith his victory has
become ours and in that faith we also are conquerors.[2]

Justification is that blessing whereby our sin has been expunged in the work of Jesus Christ. Hallelujah! Justification
is that blessing whereby the righteousness of Christ is placed
upon us so that we appear in the presence of God clothed in
it. Hallelujah! Justification is that redemptive blessing of God
whereby in Jesus Christ we have been entitled to all the blessings that Christ has secured by his death and resurrection.
Hallelujah! Amen.

Notes

1. Some may say, 'Forgive us our trespasses as we forgive those
who trespass against us.' That wording is from Luke. But in the Gospel
of Matthew 'debts' is specifically used.

2. Luther, 'A Treatise on Christian Liberty' in *Three Treatises*
(Philadelphia: Muhlenberg Press, 1947), p. 267. Also *Luther's Works*,
Vol. 31 (Philadelphia: Muhlenberg Press, 1957), pp. 357, 358.

9

Sanctification: Growing Unto God

If justification marks out the new standing we have before God in Christ, there are other blessings to be considered. Each person who has been brought to Christ has been given a new nature. That is, they have experienced regeneration. This regeneration marks the beginning of a new life – a new life which should grow and develop in a way that gives glory to God. That development is called sanctification. Sanctification relates to regeneration as growth relates to birth.

Some people are afraid of this subject because they have observed certain excesses. There are people who say, 'I have been sanctified; I am holy; I am perfect.' Now, of course, it is one thing for somebody to say 'I am perfect' of himself. It is a very different thing for his employer to say he is perfect. It is even more unusual when his wife says he is perfect! So anybody who comes up with this claim impresses us as being extravagant. He is somebody who, in the words of Paul, thinks of himself 'more highly than [he] ought' and not with 'sober judgment, in accordance with the measure of faith God has given' (Rom. 12:3). Because some people observe this and because they want by all means to avoid this overrating of oneself, they decide that it would be better not to talk about sanctification. They regard it as a dangerous subject that leads to extravagance and an inordinate appraisal of one's gifts.

Yet this is not the right solution. The way to avoid exaggerated claims is not to ignore the subject. Rather, it is to examine it in the light of Scripture. This we must do in any case since Scripture warns us that without sanctification 'no one will see the Lord' (Heb. 12:14), a passage that parallels the solemn admonition of our Lord that 'unless a man is born again, he cannot see the kingdom of God' (John 3:3).

Three comparisons

Three modern comparisons may help us to understand what is involved in sanctification.

Think first of a beautiful luxury automobile, in which everything has been carefully planned by a resourceful engineer and lovingly handcrafted by skilful mechanics. From one end to the other everything is beautifully adjusted for service and comfort. The owner is justifiably proud of this splendid machine. But now imagine that this car is stolen, driven recklessly at excessive speed and involved in a head-on collision. What have we got now? A piece of junk on the side of the road! The chassis is warped, the body is bent out of shape, the glass is shattered, the leather is cut to shreds. What has not been damaged on impact has been ruined by the ensuing fire. 'It is a total write-off,' says the insurance adjuster, 'Tow it out of here.'

But now suppose that a highly skilled craftsman should take hold of this mess of twisted metal and proceed to rebuild the car according to the original design? With infinite patience and consummate dexterity he proceeds to straighten what has been twisted, replace what has been ruined, refurbish what has been seared. Ultimately the car is restored to its pristine splendour, its engine purring like a kitten, its chrome and body gleaming, every part running smoothly. 'It is as good as new!' one might exclaim.

'Even better,' the mechanic would say, 'because of the great amount of individual attention bestowed on every part!' Sanctification may be compared to the work of that mechanic, with the understood qualification that the illustration deals with an inanimate object while sanctification applies to a living person.

Imagine, in the second place, a stately mansion set in the midst of beautifully kept grounds. Nothing was spared to make this house attractive, comfortable and durable inside and out. But it has fallen on evil days. For lack of upkeep, the property has steadily deteriorated, bushes have invaded what was once a lush lawn. The roof has been pierced, and water has damaged the inside. Squirrels have found their way into the home and caused incredible havoc. Termites have eaten into the beams and joists. Even the foundation has been weakened for lack of care. Inside the furniture has steadily deteriorated and piles of junk and refuse have built up. Now imagine that a skilled architect takes matters in hand. He sends a crew of workers to reclaim the grounds from their wild condition. He repairs everything that has been ruined. Weekly he sends trucks to remove the junk and the termite-infested wood. He brings in new furniture and luxurious carpets. Gradually he restores the dwelling to its pristine splendour. This too may be illustrative of sanctification, with the same precaution as in the previous example that we are dealing with inanimate objects instead of living persons.

Finally, take the case of the patient dying of cancer. This insidious disease has extended its noxious tentacles throughout the body. Abnormal growths have developed at many points, slowly choking life out of vital organs. Investigative surgery has revealed the extent of the damage and the surgeons have said 'Close the incision. The sickness is too far advanced, there is nothing we can do now. It is just a matter of time!' But now suppose that a master surgeon takes the patient in hand and finds ways of arresting the progress of the disease, renewing the energies of life, and removing the growths that are impeding the proper function of the body. Out of this treatment a new person emerges, once again full of life and vigour. We say, 'This is a miracle! Nobody could have expected this!' But this is a small thing compared with the greater miracle of regeneration – sanctification.

With these illustrations as a background, let us proceed to delineate certain features of sanctification.

Negative and positive

Sanctification is the work of God, in concurrence with the renewed will and energy of the Christian, which secures growth, development and maturity in the life and personality of the regenerate. It involves a negative and a positive part.

The negative part consists in bringing to nought or reducing to helplessness those elements in our being, nature, disposition and character which are alien to the will of God. When God regenerates a person he reorients the will; he implants a new governing disposition within the soul. But this implantation does not mean that God provides the full development at once. Therefore, there is a work of grace by which that which has been damaged, distorted, twisted and mangled by virtue of the presence of sin is discarded and the person is re-created to glorify God.

In terms of the illustrations provided above, we might say that certain parts of the car which have been damaged beyond repair as well as foreign elements which have intruded into the mechanism must be removed. In the house, termite-infested beams and boards must be carted away as well as some of the junk that has cluttered the inside. The cancer patient must submit to surgery so that the worst centres of infection might be eradicated. 'Whatever belongs to [our] earthly nature' must be put to death (Col. 3:5; cf. Rom. 8:13).

This process of 'mortification' is often painful, as is the removal of a tumour, but we should not resent it, no more than the man with a house full of junk should resent the trash collector!

Sanctification does not deprive us of worthwhile things.

Sometimes 'we hold on to things for dear life,' thinking they are valuable, but they are not really worthwhile. There are people who talk about making sacrifices for God. But what God asks us to give up are really the things we ought not to hold onto. They are the things we ought to let go, things that do not really matter, that do not help us on our way toward God, but hamper us, weigh us down and paralyse us. The work of God is a great boon. So, far from being afraid of sanctification and fearing that somehow it is going to be terribly costly and ruin our lives – as if God were in the business of taking all the fun out of life – we will find on the contrary that God is in the business of making our lives effective, enjoyable and useful in preparation for the life to come (Rom. 12:2).

There is a positive part as well, a renewing that God himself has undertaken. He wants to develop the new life. So in contrast to this mortification, there is a 'vivification,' a development of life as a new principle of existence within the soul.

In Christ we are a new creation, but this creation is not inanimate. It is organic; it develops; it grows; it bears fruit. It is like a tree which starts from seed, sprouts under the ground and then out of the ground, expands and eventually produces branches, leaves and fruit. So is the life of God coursing within the regenerate. It develops, enlarges and strengthens itself. It dislodges and displaces the appetites of natural, sinful humanity.

In presenting this truth the Bible uses such lofty and sublime language that we are stunned. It says that we are 'transformed into his [Christ's] likeness with ever-increasing glory' (2 Cor. 3:18). It says that we are 'being renewed in knowledge in the image of [our] Creator' (Col. 3:10). This fills us with joy. Think of the house full of junk. Somebody says, 'I am glad to come in and help you with this; I am going to come every week and take some of your junk to the dump. But I am not going to leave your house empty. I am going to bring in fine antiques, attractive curtains and nice oriental carpets.' You would say, 'How wonderful! This is really a good friend. How happy I will be to see all my junk go, and all those great and good things take their place in my house!' But this is precisely what God is doing with us.

Think of the patient dying with cancer. Now instead of the melancholy perspective of ever-greater retrenchments with ever-increasing pain, a new prospect is open which involves life, health, strength, and ever-enlarging activity and usefulness. Once again we say: 'How wonderful! Praise the Lord!' These are precisely the terms that come to our lips when we think of the nature of sanctification.

Seek sanctification
Regeneration is monergistic. That is, God is the sole agent. He acts according to his own sovereign will. He does not consult us to see whether we are willing to be regenerated, but he sovereignly begets us unto newness of life (James 1:18). This is parallel to the experience of birth in which the baby has nothing to say about his or her conception, and very little about his or her appearance in the land of the living.

Sanctification, on the other hand, is synergistic. That is, God wants to associate us with himself in accomplishing this work. He has not said, 'I am going to clean your junky house up by myself. When you come back you will find it entirely free of all the things that are unworthy.' God has said, 'I want you to have a part in this great work. I want you to bring your will into conformity with my will. I want you to yield yourself to the life I have implanted in you.' Instead of doing the work by himself, without taking account of our will, co-operation and labours, God involves us as co-laborers with him, in the same way in which in the propagation of the gospel God involves human beings as fellow-workers (1 Cor. 3:9). God involves us in the cultivation of our spiritual life and the development of our sanctification.

Sometimes we wonder about this. We may even lament about it, because we may feel that if God were doing it by himself he would do a much better job than we can. We say, 'Lord, why do you wait for me on this? Why don't you take me right into the aeroplane and fly me over the mountain, instead of making me plod along the painful upward road with all its difficulties and dangers? I seem to be so clumsy and sometimes so slow!' Yet this is how God operates, regardless of our questions. He wants us involved. He wants us to be active participants.

This is in keeping with the sovereign counsel of God in almost everything. When God inspired the Scripture he did not do it in isolation from us. He used men and women with their own capacities, language, realm of ideas and ways of expressing themselves; controlling everything, however, so that in the end Scripture was the precise expression of what God wanted to say. The marks of humanity, though not its errors, are present on every page of Scripture. So also in the Christian life. After God has called us to himself and sovereignly regenerated us, he wants us involved in sanctification. Therefore, there is this exhortation: 'Be holy; without holiness no one will see the Lord' (Heb. 12:14).

God wills our sanctification (1 Thess. 4:3). And he wills our involvement in the process – not for us to earn merits, not for us to gain a special acceptance with him (for that would becloud the doctrine of justification), but that the marvels of his grace in our renewed personalities may become apparent as we work and act and stand before God as responsible agents. We are not like pieces of wood that are being sculptured in a certain way or pieces of stone that are transported in a truck but which do nothing themselves.

Sanctification is progressive. Someone known to have fits of anger should not expect that because he or she is regenerate, he or she will now be sweet and mild in all circumstances. The temper will still be there, but now it can and must be controlled. Similarly, an alcoholic who is brought to faith does not by that fact suddenly lose his taste for alcohol or his inability to control himself after he has started drinking. There is simply another principle brought in: God's help to assist in the struggle. The struggle does not disappear. But now, instead of fighting alone and fighting a losing battle, the alcoholic is empowered to fight and triumph by the grace of God.

Some will ask, however, 'Can't we attain perfection? Isn't it God's will that we should be delivered from every remnant of sin?' The answer to this question is related to the way in which we define perfection. If we define it as 'absolute conformity to the pattern that God has set for our lives, complete obedience to the full measure of the divine commandments,' including 'love the Lord your God with all your heart and with all your soul and with all your mind' (Matt. 22:37), it will be apparent at once that nobody does attain to it in this life. Who would dare say, 'I am as perfect as Jesus'? The very presumption of such a statement would constitute an immediate proof that the claim was unfounded!

Relatively late in his career Paul disclaimed having attained to perfection (Phil. 3:12). Would anyone rashly affirm that he or she had achieved beyond the great apostle?

In order to fit the claims to the experienced reality, there are those who redefine perfection in terms of something that we can reach, but in the process they undercut the majesty and the depth of God's law! They lower the standards in order to fit the competitors! This may sometimes be desirable in human affairs, but it will not do where the character of God and his will are at stake.

But then what shall we say of passages like 1 John 3:6-9 and 5:18, that appear to teach that one who is born of God does not and cannot sin? The very sweeping character of these passages, applying as they do to any true Christian and not merely to some advanced saints and asserting that sin is not merely avoidable but actually impossible, would make it evident that John is here speaking of a special category of sin rather than of every sinful act. This impression is reinforced by the context of 1 John 5, in which John distinguishes between 'a sin that does not lead to death' and 'a sin that leads to death' for which even prayer cannot avail (vv. 16, 17). The sin which one truly born of God cannot commit might be identified as the sin of complete apostasy, a total revulsion against the gospel after exposure to the fullness of its light.[1] What 1 John 3 and 5 tell us is that the regenerate cannot commit this kind of sin because God keeps them from it. They are passages on the perseverance of God with the saints, not statements on perfectionism.

Why struggle?

Sometimes we wonder why God permits us to struggle so long in the life of sanctification. One answer is surely that sanctification brings us face to face with *the reality of our sin*. In sanctification we are exposed to an increasing understanding of the corruption of our heart. We do not discover that all at once, even though at the point of conversion there is often a dramatic conviction of sin which the Holy Spirit brings about. Generally it is only in the process of growth in the Lord that we are led to probe into the reality and depth of our corruption.

The illustrations of the wrecked car, the broken-down house and the cancer patient were meant to reflect something of the gravity of our predicament as sinners.

To be sure, we are made aware of human sinfulness when

we consider other Christians. We are much more able to see their defects than we are to see our own. But sometimes the reality is so striking that, even with the desire we have to excuse ourselves, we cannot help recognizing that it is true of us as well. We say, 'That person is ambitious.' But suddenly we see that we have roots of ambition in our own hearts. We say, 'Why is she so critical?' We suddenly realize that we too are very critical. (We are critical of critical people, if nothing else.) 'Why are people so narrow?' we ask. Then we realize that we too are also often lacking in forbearance.

So the life of sanctification is a life of painful discoveries. In fact, the more we grow in sanctification, the more likely we are to discover how very bad we are. This is apparent in the career of the apostle Paul. In 1 Corinthians 15, Paul, toward the beginning of his ministry, said in a rather humble way that he was 'the least of the apostles' (v. 9). This was a remarkable statement, because Paul is one apostle that most of us remember. If we mention three apostles, they will probably be Paul, Peter and John. We do not often think of Thaddeus, Bartholomew or the others! Somebody who says that the apostle Paul was less than some of the others would seemingly be out of order. But this is what *Paul* says! He places himself last in this category.

A few years later in the life of Paul we come to the letter to the Ephesians. In that epistle the apostle calls himself 'less than the least of all God's people,' that is, the least of all believers (Eph. 3:8). That is an even stranger statement, for we would say that by this time the apostle was surely one of the greatest believers. He was one in whom the grace of God had appeared in a most signal manner. He was a totally unlikely candidate even for election, yet he had become one of the most effective missionaries. Still he says in Ephesians that he is the least of Christians, not worthy of the grace of God.

Finally, at the very close of his career, in 1 Timothy, we find him saying, 'Here is a trustworthy saying that deserves full acceptance: Christ Jesus came into the world to save sinners – of whom I am the worst' (1 Tim. 1:15). What does this mean? It means that as the life of grace was enlarging within the apostle, his own self-esteem diminished. In getting closer to the Lord and more fully under the control of the Holy Spirit he perceived even more clearly wherein he fell short.

Another reason why God does not perfect us at once is because of *the interest he has in us as persons*. He does not deal with us as with pieces of wood or stone, but as rational agents.

In a sense God has the joy parents have in seeing the first steps of a child. Newborn deer run as fast as their parents as soon as they are born. But there is something especially tender and moving in the spectacle of parents who guide the steps of their children. They see them stumble somewhat, but they are there to support them. Parents who love their children have a sense of blessing as they see these children grow and watch their progress. In a similar way, God takes joy in our progress. Obviously, he does not take joy in our defeats or rebellion or the way we sometimes abandon and betray him. But he takes joy in the way in which we take hold of that life that he has provided, and work under his guidance and by his power to struggle with him and for him in the conquest of evil.

Means of grace

To promote our sanctification God has provided means of grace by which the life of the Spirit is enhanced. One of these is mentioned in the famous prayer of our Lord in John 17, in which Jesus said, 'Sanctify them by the truth; your word is truth' (v.17). He shows that sanctification is promoted by the *cultivation* of *Scripture,* not only as a book out of which we are going to draw propositions (though it contains propositional truth), but as spiritual food which is able to renew us and cause us to apprehend more fully the blessings and grace of God. We need to remain closely attached to the Scriptures in order that our lives may grow. If we do not have the Scriptures, we are going to be retarded children. We deplore retardation at the human level, even in a physical way. How much more regrettable this is spiritually! But in order not to be retarded we need to have the Word of God challenge us day by day, week by week.

God also has provided *prayer* as a means of grace, because through prayer we can establish lines of communication with him. It seems strange that God should have to admonish us to pray, for it is an honour for us to be allowed to come into his presence and make our requests known. Yet this is what the Scripture has to tell us. 'Pray continually,' said the apostle Paul (1 Thess. 5:17); 'Watch and pray so that you will not fall into temptation,' says our Lord Jesus Christ (Matt. 26:41). Prayer is presented, not only as a privilege, which it is, but also as a duty. For it is in prayer that the life of holiness will develop. Things which are unworthy will be sloughed off, and things that are God's will for us will be enhanced.

Christian fellowship is a means of grace. In the United States we tend to be overly individualistic. There are some areas of the world where people function perhaps too much in terms of larger units, like the family, or the tribe, or the state; but in the United States we are extremely individualistic. We want to emphasize each person for himself or herself, each one as a distinct object of interest. Surely there are some good reasons for doing this, but we need to recognize that God has not called us to live the life of Robinson Crusoe at the spiritual level. There are no spiritual islands. We are called to be a people of God, not separate individuals. When God sent the disciples, he sent them two by two. He did not send them to their work in isolation.

Most of the time we need the support of other believers. We need to be strengthened and comforted. We need to be edified by one another. We need to be challenged and watched. We need to help others when they are about to fall. Sanctification is a life in which God's people function as a family – love one another, support one another, help one another. Therefore, in the very context in which Hebrews says, 'Be holy; without holiness no one will see the Lord,' it also says, 'Let us not give up meeting together' (Heb. 10:25). When we think that we are so great, so good, so spiritual that we do not need our brothers and sisters in Christ, that is the time when we are about to fall. God has decreed that we will stand when we are with his other children, as members of his family, and not just by ourselves.

God has provided *the sacraments* as a means of grace, because they signify in a moving manner what he has done for us. They are signs of his blessing and tokens of his immeasurable love. Baptism and the Lord's Supper seal and certify to our consciousness the benefits which accrue to us from the work of Christ. They help stabilize and develop the life of the Spirit in us.

Yearn to be holy

It behooves us who rejoice in our redemption, bask in the glory of justification by faith and thrill to our adoption as children of God – it behooves us with earnestness and zeal to seek that life of conformity and obedience to the will of God that alone is pleasing in his sight.

Let us not be reconciled with evil. Let us not say, 'I am a sinner, but I just can't help it. It really doesn't matter what I'm doing in the end.' Let us say rather, 'God has called me to holiness. His will for me is not that I should be a defeated

Christian, who lies always on the side of the road, buffeted and overcome by the power of evil both from within and without. His will is that I should be holy. I should be dedicated to him. So long as I live I should move forward toward that goal he has established. I should be renewed in the image of Christ. God's will is to take that miserable wreck that lies on the side of the road and change it bit by bit until gradually, by the act of the supreme mechanic, he produces a splendid new thing beautiful, serviceable, where everything works; where every button controls something in the proper way, where nothing is amiss. I want to work with him on this project.

'God's will is to take that rundown, junk-filled house in the midst of weed- and brush-infested grounds and to rebuild and refurbish it so that it will be a palatial mansion in a lovely garden. I want to work with him on his project.

'God's will is to take this cancer-ridden patient, paralysed in his vital functions and wracked with pain and anguish, and to renew, invigorate, restore and prepare him for life everlasting. I want to work with him on this project.'

How we must yearn for sanctification! When we study the grace of God, we must be moved to request of the Lord that he should take those unworthy things out of our lives, renew us into his image and use us, trophies of his grace, for the blessing of others. Those who see us should not say, 'Here is another piece of junk. I never expected more.' Rather, they should say, 'Here is somebody in whom God's grace is at work. It is unmistakable. I would like to have a life like that.' Unless we do this, the witness of our lips will not be strong. We may tell the truth, but the truth will never be convincing when it is not backed up by our lives.

I would exhort you to 'Be holy,' for 'without holiness no one will see the Lord.' And may God himself, who by his mercy has richly blessed us in so many ways, add also this blessing: That we may triumph in temptation, be strong in the Lord to do his will, be renewed in conformity to his image, and glorify his holy name in the presence of this world and even in the face of Satan.

I conclude with a stanza of Charles Wesley, perhaps my favourite of all that he has written:

> He wills that I should holy be.
> Who can withstand His will?
> *The counsel of His grace in me*
> He surely shall fulfil.[2]

Notes

1. Other passages that deal with this kind of offence are: Matt. 12:31, 32; Mk. 3:28, 29; Heb. 6:4-6; 10:26-31; 2 Peter 2; 1 John 2:18, 19.

2. *The Poetical Works of John and Charles Wesley* (London: Epworth Press, 1969), Vol. 2, p. 243.

10

Predestination and the Great Commission

We have set out our case that if we are to give God proper glory, we must do justice to what the Bible says about predestination. Some people, however, will object and allege that predestination and the Great Commission are mutually exclusive. And if their objection is valid, it will undermine our contentions about predestination.

We must look into the objection in a little more detail. It runs like this – if you really believe in predestination (that God has chosen some and bypassed others), this will cut the nerve of missionary activity. In effect, we would have to repudiate Calvinism if we are to carry out the command that our Lord has given us. I do concede that there are some people (let us call them hyper-Calvinists) who have distorted predestination to excuse their own lack of fervour in the service to which the Lord has called them. I would emphasize that this is a distortion. When predestination is pressed into service as a repudiation of the Great Commission and the zeal we should have for bringing the gospel to lost souls, then a most disastrous development has taken place. This drastically misunderstands what Scripture means (and what proper Calvinists mean) when they say that God has foreordained some to salvation and bypassed others who are reproved for their sins.

The first misunderstanding
The reason why the two have been thought to be antagonistic may be summarized by four major misunderstandings. First,

some people reason that if God has not elected certain individuals, then nothing we can do will lead them to salvation and therefore there is no use in our bringing the gospel to them. We might as well stay at home and enjoy our TV.

This line of reasoning is completely fallacious from the start, because God's electing decision is secret. He has not communicated it to us. I would like to stress in the most emphatic manner that we have no right to view people as non-elect merely because they are not yet saved. Who seemed to be a better candidate for being non-elect than the apostle Paul? He was so bad that even the church at Jerusalem, which was used to seeing great outpourings of divine power and had actually had three thousand converts in one meeting, doubted that God would really have stooped to reach him. He had been a persecutor of the church and was considered the most nefarious enemy of the Jerusalem believers. The church was freezing him out. Indeed, if it had not been for the courage, vision, understanding and compassion of Barnabas, Paul might very well have been turned off by the coldness of those he wished to join. As it turned out, Paul was used as one of the greatest servants of God of all time.

How about the people we reach? Are we able to say, 'This person is even worse than Paul'? I doubt it. But even if he or she were worse than Paul, that still gives us no ground for thinking that somehow that one is non-elect. The very fact that you know this person – the very fact that you are in contact with this person, the very fact that there is a burden upon your heart for this person – ought to be an indication that quite possibly, even probably, he or she has been picked by God. Probably God wants to use you to reach that one and thus manifest the purpose of election. The idea that there are some people who are not elect ought to give us absolutely no support in the thought that somehow we can spare ourselves the trouble of reaching out with the good news of the gospel.

In my judgment there is not an ounce of truth in this reasoning, and the people who present it either do not understand the doctrine of predestination or are unaware that it is a distortion. A proper understanding, far from discouraging us from presenting the gospel to people who are presently lost, ought actually to encourage us to do so.

A second misunderstanding

The second contention by which people think that predestination and the Great Commission are in opposition is this: If God has elected certain people, he is going to bring them into his fold himself. Therefore, we do not need to exert ourselves, because nothing we might fail to do would foil God's purposes.

This reasoning also has no strength, because it does not take account of the fact, very clearly taught in Scripture, that the purposes of God are fulfilled through means, and that the means God has elected for the salvation of people is the preaching of the gospel. Without the preaching of the gospel we cannot expect the election of God to take effect. When God elected some people to be saved, he also elected the means by which they should be saved. He elected preachers to proclaim the message and the power of his Holy Spirit to melt their resistance. Upon hearing the message, they manifest election by repentance and faith. To attempt to disconnect the end, which is the salvation God has foreordained, from the means, which in this case is the presentation of the gospel to those who have not yet heard it or to those who have heard it but not yet accepted it, is a most mischievous misunderstanding of God's ways.

God has given us a very plain command. So we are in no position to say, 'We will disregard the command because we do not know how it is going to be fulfilled.' We do not perceive the way in which God is carrying out his purpose of election, and it is not our business to inquire how God carries it out. It is our business to be obedient to the command God gives. If anybody says, 'The Lord doesn't need me; I can just as well go my way without concern for the evangelistic and missionary endeavour; God has foreordained people and they will be saved whether I put my hand to it or not,' that person drastically distorts the doctrine of election.

This is, in fact, pretty well what happened when the great missionary William Carey expressed his desire to evangelize pagans. He encountered a very strange objection, one so strange that I do not suppose there are many people today who present it. People told him that the Great Commission was only for the eleven apostles, that it was carried out in their time and that, in the same way in which tongues and other miraculous activities had ceased, so had the obligation to go into all the world preaching the gospel. This is so ridiculous that I do not think I need to spend much time with it. The Great Commission itself flies in the face of this outlook, Jesus said, 'I will be with you always, to the very end of the age' (Matt. 28:20). So, obviously, the Commission goes beyond the lives of the apostles.

Carey also received another objection. When old John Ryland heard Carey encourage people to reach others in distant lands, he said, 'Sit down, young man, you are a miserable enthusiast! [That is, you are claiming to possess a gift of the Spirit, which we do not have any more.] When God wants to convert the heathen he will do it without your help or mine.' This man was a hyper-Calvinist. He had failed to understand that God reaches the heathen through the ministrations of his people. This is a task which we have no right to shirk. We have no right to say, 'That doesn't apply to me.' On the contrary, it does apply, and the fact that God has elected people from all nations ought to be an encouragement to us to go to those nations to make disciples. Indeed, we should even learn new tongues so that in the end a great multitude of all tribes and *tongues* and nations can be gathered around the throne to glorify God.

The company of the elect is not going to be a narrow, Anglo-Saxon company. It is going to be a great company of people derived from all parts of this world. It is through missions that these people are drawn by the gracious, elective purpose of God into fellowship with Jesus Christ through whom salvation is received. Therefore, there is no force at all in the contention that if God has elected people, we do not need to worry whether they will be saved or not; they will be saved without our help. On the contrary, it may very well be through our prayers, witness, and zeal for missionary and evangelistic endeavours that the elective purpose of God for them will be accomplished.

A third misunderstanding

A third argument advanced against predestination and the Great Commission runs as follows: If God has only chosen some, we are not in a position to offer Christ to all. In order to be universal, the offer must be grounded in a universal provision. Consequently, if God has ordained salvation and Christ has purchased salvation only for some, that is, those who will be redeemed, we cannot in good conscience say to everyone, 'Believe on the Lord Jesus Christ and you will be saved.' (Acts 16:31).

This question gives considerable anguish to many well-meaning people who feel that somehow the doctrines of grace must undercut the sincerity of the gospel offer. What is assumed here erroneously is that in order to have a proper offer you need to have what I call a co-extensive provision. That is, a provision must be set up in advance which is as large as the field of persons reached by the offer. It is that principle, it seems to me, that is at the root of the objection.

I would suggest that in our experience very few offers have this fullest provision. Suppose that in this week's paper there will be an announcement in which a large company will advertise some major appliances, say, refrigerators. I ask, Is the company sincere in making this offer? If so, shall I conclude that since this advertisement appears in the paper, which is distributed perhaps to 600,000 people, that there are 600,000 refrigerators of this type in the company's warehouses? Obviously this is a ridiculous proposition. If the company ran its business this way, they would fail before the month is over, because they would have thousands of refrigerators they could not sell. What does the company do when it makes an offer like that? Assuming that this is a good refrigerator and the price is favourable, I presume it stores a certain number of refrigerators so that the customers who come will receive one if they want it. The supply will be adequate for the people who come forward to avail themselves of the offer.

If the company had only one such refrigerator, then you would have what is called a 'come on.' It would be an offer of something without any real intention of selling – just a trick to get some people into their store where they could then be talked into buying a television set or something else. That would not be a genuine offer, because the company would not be intending to provide refrigerators for people who would ask for them. But so long as the customers who come can get refrigerators at the price stated, there is no objection to be raised with Sears concerning the number of refrigerators stored. That is the company's business. It is not the customers' concern.

To have a genuine offer you do not need a co-extensive provision. All you need is a situation in which if somebody complies with the terms of the offer, what has been promised will in fact be provided. That is all anyone who hears an offer has a right to expect.

So also with the offer of the gospel. As far as the offer of the gospel is concerned, there is not ground for objecting, 'Did Christ actually die for every man, woman and child? Did God choose every man, woman and child in the world?' That is none of our business. The only thing needed for a well-meant offer is to be able to say, 'Come to Jesus Christ, and you will find that he has died for you. Repent! Believe!' In all the history of mankind there is not a single case of anybody who came to repentance and faith in the terms God has indicated but who then heard God say, 'Sorry, this gospel is not intended for you.' How do I know that? I know that because Jesus said, 'Whoever comes to me I will never drive away' (John 6:37). I believe Jesus. Therefore, I can preach and offer the gospel of salvation without any qualms whatever. I have no fear that somebody responding in repentance and faith will ever find that his or her name is not written in the book of life.

What makes me even more confident in this is that nobody will respond unless God first draws him or her. Jesus said, 'No one can come to me unless the Father who sent me draws him' (John 6:44). So when repentance and faith appear they are an indication that God has drawn that person. The gospel message does not compel us to say, 'Christ died for *you*; God loves *you*' before we know how people will respond. The gospel is merely that Christ came to save sinners like you and me. Therefore, however great your sin may be, however severe your burden of guilt or deep your expectation of judgment, there is a refuge in Jesus Christ if you will come to him. What kind of provision God has made is his business. All we need know is that he has made full provision for all who will come.

A fourth misunderstanding

Some people have said, 'Well, anyway, all great evangelists and missionaries have been Arminians.' That is not true, but I am not going to provide you with a long list of names of Calvinistic evangelists and missionaries. Instead, I want to talk about one of the great pioneers in missions, William Carey.

Carey was a 'particular' Baptist, the word 'particular' emphasizing that in his denomination people believed in particular redemption. They were supporters of what I like to call 'definite atonement.' This man seemed to have very little prospects for Christian work for he had been raised in rather poor surroundings and had very few means by which to pursue an education. He was a cobbler and a weaver. But Carey began to study the Scriptures and, as a result, was seized by a concern for the condition of the heathen. He sensed very deeply that the church ought not to remain at ease while the heathen were unreached. Indeed, they were being reached for financial and commercial enterprises, but very few people were doing anything for them in terms of Christian work. When Carey began to speak about this he received the rebukes I spoke of earlier. But his sense of the lostness of the heathen kept pressing in on him.

One day he was called to preach a sermon at a gathering of Baptist ministers. He preached on Isaiah's words: 'Enlarge the place of your tent...lengthen your cords' (Isa. 54:2, 3). Like Carey's shoes (that he always repaired in pairs), this sermon had two points. First, expect great things from God. This was predestination. Second, attempt great things for God. Sometimes people tell that story and invert the points. But Carey had it right: first, 'expect,' then, 'attempt.' There was a man called Andrew Fuller who encouraged Carey to put his thoughts in writing, as a result of which he published a pamphlet entitled, 'An Enquiry Into the Obligations of

Christians to Use Means for the Conversion of the Heathen.'
It appeared in 1792. In it Carey examined the objections to
the missionary and evangelistic endeavours, dismissed them,
and then proceeded to list all the places in the world he knew
of with their populations and what kind of religions they had.
Carey produced a table with all kinds of geographical terms
that are today quite antiquated: e.g., Zeeland, Funen, Arroe,
Langeland, Laland, Falster, Mona, Alsen, Femerman, to read
only one page. In many of those cases I do not even know
what lands he was talking about. But he gathered up the whole
population of the world in this way, claiming that it contained
then about 770 million people, more than half of whom had
never been reached with the gospel. He pressed this task upon
the church. Indeed, he put himself at the disposal of his
brethren to be sent himself as a missionary to India in order
to proclaim the good news of Christ there. Listen to the way
he describes what a minister should be.

A Christian minister is a person who in a peculiar sense is not
his own. He is the servant of God and therefore ought to be
wholly devoted to him. By entering on that sacred office he
solemnly undertakes to be always engaged, as much as possible,
in the Lord's work and not to choose his own pleasure, or
employment, or pursue the ministry as something that is to
subserve his own ends, or interests, or as a kind of by-work.
He engages to go where God pleases, and to do, or endure
what he sees fit to command, or call him to, in the exercise of
his function. He virtually bids farewell to friends, pleasures,
and comforts, and stands in readiness to endure the greatest
sufferings in the work of his Lord, and Master. It is inconsistent
for ministers to please themselves with thoughts of a numerous
auditory, cordial friends, a civilized country, legal protection,
affluence, splendour, or even a competency. The slights, and
hatred of men, and even pretended friends, gloomy prisons,
and tortures, a society of barbarians of uncouth speech,
miserable accommodations in wretched wildernesses, hunger

and thirst, nakedness, weariness, and painfulness, hard work, and but little worldly encouragement, should rather be the objects of their expectation. Thus the apostles acted, in the primitive times, and endured hardness, as good soldiers of Jesus Christ; and though we live in a civilized country where Christianity is protected by law, are not called to suffer these things while we continue here, yet I question whether all are justified in staying here, while so many are perishing without means of grace in other lands. Sure I am that it is entirely contrary to the spirit of the gospel, for its ministers to enter upon it from interested motives, or with great worldly expectations. On the contrary the commission is a sufficient call to them to venture all, and, like the primitive Christians, go everywhere preaching the gospel (pp. 72, 73. Spelling modernized).

Carey went to India and by his own example and labours became an inspiration for others. So the year 1792, in which this 'Enquiry' appeared, is considered the foundational year of the modern missionary movement. But note: there is no word in all this pamphlet that is in any way inconsistent with mainline Calvinism.

And what shall we say about Charles Haddon Spurgeon, one of the most gifted and moving evangelists God was pleased to give his church in the last century? He was a very strong, five-point Calvinist. But he composed that sermon, 'Come, and Welcome to Jesus Christ,' which has been the means God used for the conversion of multitudes. Spurgeon hardly preached a sermon without giving some invitation in which people would have opportunity to manifest their response to God's call of grace. He was the means of the conversion of literally thousands, perhaps millions of persons.

The effective Word of God

Far from undermining the significance and urgency of the Great Commission, a proper understanding of the doctrine of sovereign grace actually gives a special lift and help in this respect.

It does this in two ways. First, it assures us that our witness of Jesus Christ will be effective, not in terms of our own persuasiveness, but in terms of the sovereign action of God. God has put it very clearly in Isaiah 55:10, 11:

> As the rain and the snow come down from heaven, and do not return to it without watering the earth and making it bud and flourish, so that it yields seed for the sower and bread for the eater, so is my word that goes out from my mouth: It will not return to me empty, but will accomplish what I desire and achieve the purpose for which I sent it.

There is a success in missionary endeavour which does not come from the competency or ability of the evangelist but from the promise of God. It is the Father who draws people. He draws them through the preaching of the gospel which God graciously has commissioned us to bring to human beings.

The second reason that obedience to the Great Commission is enhanced by the doctrine of sovereign grace is that, if you do not believe in sovereign grace, all that you can offer is a kind of tentative salvation. You have to say to people, 'God has done so much, but now you have to do your part in order to be saved. If you do not do that, salvation will not result and you will be lost.' The person who believes in the sovereign grace of God can say, 'God has done everything needed. Salvation is all of grace.' The invitation comes in the name of the Master who says:

'Come to me, all you who are weary and burdened, and I will give you rest' (Matt. 11:28).

'Go and make disciples of all nations, baptizing them in the name of the Father and of the Son and of the Holy Spirit' (Matt. 28:19).

'Here I am! I stand at the door and knock. If anyone hears my voice and opens the door, I will come in and eat with him and he with me' (Rev. 3:20).

We live in a world which needs people who take the Great Commission seriously. Millions are dying without the knowledge of Jesus Christ, some of them at our doors. Some of them may be our neighbours, or the grocer, or the mailman who delivers our mail day by day. Perhaps some are even people we see in church but who are not yet reached by the message of grace. Others are in distant lands, in places where the gospel has perhaps never been heard, where people would not even know what you were talking about if you would say, 'Jesus.' Can we sit at ease when so many who are the proper objects of the invitation of the grace of God have never heard of it?

11

When God Calls

In our last chapter we examined some of the objections that are put forward against the possibility of missions from a Calvinistic standpoint. I intend in this chapter to take a more positive thrust and to illustrate that the God who ordains many to salvation and bypasses others is very active in mission. He wills that his church should have the same zeal for mission and that all his people should be involved in some way in that mighty enterprise.

Let us begin in the early church in Antioch. The Holy Spirit said to its leaders: 'Set apart for me Barnabas and Saul for the work to which I have called them' (Acts 13:2). This passage represents a very crucial moment in the history of the church and particularly in the history of missions: here for the first time by the direct commandment of God an enterprise was initiated in which some people set off on a journey for no other purpose than the purpose of bringing the gospel to people who had not yet heard it. I am not denying the presence of the principle of missions in the Old Testament, notably in the case of Jonah. I am not denying either that in Acts 8 we have the great mission work of Philip who was sent off some sixty miles away from Samaria where he was mainly occupied, in order to reach out for just one person of African origin. But in Acts 13, we have a situation in which God especially sets apart a missionary party. Here people are going out for the specific purpose of doing God's work and presenting the gospel to those who have not heard. Acts 13 represents, if you want, the launching pad of Christian missions. Judging from a purely human point of view one might say, 'Big deal! Just three people leaving Seleucia on a little boat going a few miles away to Cyprus. This is hardly a conspicuous beginning.' And yet this was the start of a tremendous enterprise which God by his mercy and power carried out through the ages and which is at the heart of God's major purpose for his church. It is therefore important for us to analyse what is involved in this tremendous statement, 'set aside for me Barnabas and Saul for the work to which I have called them.' Let us do so here in terms of the parties in view.

What does this mean for God, the supreme sender? What does it reveal to us concerning God?

What did this mean for the church of Antioch, the subsidiary sender?

What did this mean for Barnabas and Saul who are being sent?

What does this mean for the heathen to whom they were sent?

What does this mean for you and me today?

Some of these points will be explored more fully than others.

What this means with respect to God?

First of all, this statement shows God's *supreme concern* for people who are lost. Sometimes people might think because God did not provide a regular means of reaching out for the heathen that he did not care, that it did not matter to him that there were vast multitudes of mankind that were being lost without receiving any kind of Divine revelation in a supernatural way so that they might be saved. But surely this is not correct and this particular moment in the history of the church shows how very much God cares. For God chose two of his most qualified servants, two of the choicest people in the whole history of the early church. He chose Paul, whom many would consider to be the superlative missionary of all times, a man prepared with consummate care, whose personality excelled in every direction, who had been one of the gospel's greatest conquests, and was so much on fire for Jesus Christ that nothing else really mattered: all the things which for others were gain he just viewed as a loss for excellency of the knowledge and of the service of Jesus Christ (Phil. 3:7,8). And at his side Barnabas who was perhaps the most compassionate figure of all the New Testament, a man always ready to sacrifice himself if in the process he could help others. It is these people that God chose for missions. Not some people who in some way or another were not able to make the grade at home! Not people who were failing in the ministry as pastors of a church, and about whom some people would say, 'Well, I guess they can't make it here, let's send them to the heathen, to somebody or other that doesn't matter.' These were the very best that the church could provide!

In a sense we really didn't need that in order to know the superlative concern of God. Because this superlative concern of God is expressed for us at a higher scale yet in the one who was the greatest missionary, even the Lord Jesus who left the blessings and glories of the presence of the Father in order to come down all the way to us in our misery, in our sin, in order to share with us, not at the level of human greatness but at the level of the little ones, the oppressed, the downtrodden, the sick, the sorrowful, and to establish the principle that is at the basis of salvation and to proclaim also a year of recovery of the Lord, liberation for the captives, healing for the diseased, renewal for all (Luke, 4:18,19). And so, when we know that the Lord Jesus cared enough to come, that God the Father cared enough to send his only Son, there is certainly no proper grounds for saying that God does not care, or that it really doesn't matter to him whether people are saved or lost. The supreme concern of God is made very manifest. It is at the very heart of the whole work of missions that God is concerned, that God cares, and that there is no sacrifice that is too great in order to carry out this task.

In this occasion also the *sovereign control* of God was made manifest. It is made plain here that God rules over the church, and he may give directives to the church which are not in line with their natural inclination. He said, 'I have called them to a certain task, I am the one who determines who will do what. Don't think that you can begin to rule and make plans and make your decisions in terms of your own human wisdom, I remain in control; this is my harvest; you are workers in the vineyard, I am the master.' This is made apparent also in that after the church of Antioch had obeyed the command of God we read that they were sent on their way by the Holy Spirit (Acts 13:4). Yes, they were also sent by the church. Yes, the elders of the church had placed their hands upon them and said, 'you are our people, and we send you and delegate you in the name of God.' But at the back of this it needed always to be remembered that God was the one who sent; God was the one at the fountainhead, at the origin of this whole movement; God was the one to whom ultimately they were to be responsible and give their account at the last day. So the task of missions is under the divine control: it is he who has the plan to be implemented, and it is our task to be obedient to him, and to respond to the intimations of the Holy Spirit so that the work may be accomplished.

What did it mean to the church of Antioch?

Let us carefully reflect upon this aspect of this passage, for perhaps we may not always sufficiently consider what this message meant for the church. The whole situation is introduced by giving us an inventory of their ministerial resources. Five names are given, two that are familiar to us, one very much so, the name of Paul. And the name of

Barnabas is familiar because he appears several times in the New Testament. The other three are never otherwise mentioned or known.

Simeon called Niger: the word *Niger* in Latin means black, so perhaps he was somebody who came from Africa. One of the great things in Antioch was that there was quite a mixture of races in that great city, and Christianity managed to have its impact and its appeal to the people of all races.

Lucius of Cyrene: Cyrene is a city of Africa from which Simon who carried Jesus' cross behind him had come (Luke 23:26). So here was another African who had a place in the ministry.

And then Manaen who had been brought up with Herod the tetrarch. That seems to be a questionable qualification for ministerial service, because Herod the tetrarch was hardly a commendable person in Christian terms. To be brought up with Herod the tetrarch would lead to all kinds of undisciplined behaviour, all kinds of inappropriate approaches, perhaps a taste of luxury which a Christian might not be allowed to continue to indulge. Surely such background might provide training for competent teachers and instructors, but probably not a very high level of moral life. Yet God had been able to reach out for this man and transform his life and make use of the excellent tools that he had received in his youth. So he too had a place in ministry.

Then the message came. The church had, as is appropriate, a time of special spiritual retreat in which they were fasting and praying, seeking the Lord's will. It was a church that had been exceptionally successful in what was perhaps the third largest city of the world, with thousands of teeming people in need there, and they were prepared to meet that need. We have to remember that it is in Antioch that the disciples were first called Christians (Acts 11:26). There for the first time Christianity came out as distinctive, something profoundly different from Judaism, something that demanded another name. Antioch was in a sense the second capital city of Christianity. So these people were dependent upon the power of God and his Spirit to carry on their mandate. They were prayerfully seeking to find out what this mandate might be. And then it came, like a bolt of lightning, 'Set apart for me Barnabas and Saul for the work to which I have called them. You are not going to have them any more, I am taking them away from you for something else.' Now just try to figure out how you would have reacted if you were a member of the church of Antioch and this message came out. I don't know who may be Barnabas and Saul in your midst. Surely your pastor would be one of them, and furthermore some other person on whom you rely heavily for ministry, for nurture, for the exposition of the Word of God. And now suddenly God wants to take them both away!

There must have been some people who thought: 'Lord, you may have Barnabas, but we want Paul; we need him, he is the man just for the hour, he is the man for a city like Antioch, he is a man who has an understanding of the Old Testament Scripture that surpasses anything that anybody ever had around here, and we need that kind of a man in the city; we need this masterful and creative grasp of revealed truth which challenges us Sunday after Sunday. Of course we appreciate Barnabas; he was a great man of God to perceive the plight of the heathen and to help us in our time of need, and perhaps the heathen need him at some other place; so you may have him, but we want to keep Paul.' There may have been some other people who might have said: 'O.K. Lord, you can have Paul, but we want Barnabas. We realize that Paul cannot be a man of one church; his greatness exceeds even our church; he belongs to the world, so send him, Lord. Besides he is a little rough at times and once in a while he tends even to rock the boat in our church. Take him, Lord, and use him in the great ministry that you have. We want Barnabas; we want that man with tender heart, with loving hands, with gracious smile, always ready to help those who are in need. We can't get along without him. For a long time we got along without Paul. When Barnabas was here alone, everything was going along well; so now you take Paul, and we keep Barnabas.'

But that was not the message. God had said, 'Give me Barnabas *and* Paul.' Whoever thought that mission could be carried on with the people or the resources that we don't need? Whoever thought you could have what is called a missionary barrel, in which you put your rejects and carry on with all the things that you are used to? At the very start God really cut the church to the quick, and from this church in Antioch he demanded a staggering sacrifice. They had to give up the two most qualified people they had. But they did not disobey the heavenly vision. They prayed and laid their hands on these two men who had been the ministers of so much blessing for the church, and they sent them on their way. I dare say, there wasn't one dry eye in the house! They trusted that God would continue to bless them. Paul and Barnabas would continue to be under the loving care and support of the church of Antioch.

What did this mean for Paul and Barnabas?
It meant that they sensed in a very special way that they were under the direct control of God. They had been placed by divine appointment in fellowship with one another. How wonderful it is that God should be careful to have people working in teams for the work of missions. A few years ago I made a lengthy journey around the world looking at missionary fields and I saw some missionaries that were stranded, who were alone; and being alone it seems to me that they deteriorated, they were permitted in some way to feel lonely and lost in the midst of a foreign culture and

sometimes this had damaging effects on their own attitude toward the people that they were called upon to evangelise. I saw one person who was so grievously burdened in this way, perhaps psychologically, but perhaps spiritually, that she had come to loathe the very people in the midst of which she was a missionary. I must say I blame the missionary society to have permitted that woman to remain alone for more than a year because her original companion had some problems medically and was withdrawn and nobody was sent for a whole year. This had most damaging effects.

Not so with God; he called two people. Even the apostle Paul with his tremendous spiritual maturity seemed always surrounded by companions in one way or another. And mission is a formidable task that demands companionship; it demands mutual support; it demands teamwork. People who are alone can scarcely be expected to carry out this work. It is a work that is demanding because not only does it call, as the preaching of the gospel ordinarily does, for an application of the truth of the Scripture to our own culture, it demands that someone should make a connection with another culture, a culture with which one must identify in every way that is possible except ways that are a violation of the law of God. And one must interpret the gospel in terms of that other culture in order to present the Lord Jesus Christ in his grace in ways that are suitable for the people who are to be reached.

What does this call mean for the heathen?

Surely it means that God is concerned. God didn't care just for the Jews, but he has elect people in all the nations of the world. There is no group about whom we can say, 'Well, God doesn't care about these, these are the dregs. Who wants to do anything for them?' God shows the breadth of his all-encompassing mercy. So this occasion in Antioch was a great day for the heathen; God had remembered them; God was concerned for them. This concern which God has and which reaches out into the uttermost parts of the earth must be echoed and reflected in the heart of the Christian.

What does this mean for you and for me?

This is not just something that happened over nineteen hundred years ago. God has prepared us for a task, he has called us to a ministry. This ministry must be accomplished in fellowship with his people, not by freelancers who move all over the earth without any kind of provision for continuity and perpetuity in their work. God requires men and women who are moving out in the fellowship of God's people, who are related to the church, who sense their moorings in the congregation they have left. God has prepared each of us for a task. There is no Christian who can say, 'I am not a missionary.' There are places that you can reach that nobody else can reach. There are people for whom you can work that nobody else can invite in the same way in God's name. We have a task to accomplish. The Lord says, 'Set aside for me this one, that one, for the work to which I have called them.' May the Lord grant that with utmost seriousness and with the sense of the solemn presence of our Lord, we may commit ourselves even as Isaiah committed himself, and say, 'Lord, here I am, send me' (Isaiah 6:8).

12

Freedom and Law

No believer is his or her own master. We are all under orders from our Saviour, the Lord Jesus Christ. Not least, we are to share his passion for the lost.

'But where does that leave my freedom?' someone may say. There is no doubt that freedom strikes a responsive chord in the hearts of men. Many Christians will echo the famous words of Patrick Henry: 'Give me liberty or give me death.' For we know that we are created for liberty, created not to be enslaved or yoked or under the unfair and unjust dominion of anyone else, but to be free. The subject of freedom is one which challenges the hearts of men. Almost every country celebrates its national holiday on the anniversary of the day on which it acquired freedom.

But freedom has a much deeper meaning than in the political sphere alone. This is not to downgrade the significance of political freedom, but to stress that political freedom is only one aspect of the total life of freedom which God has provided for us and to which God challenges us in his Word.

The nature of freedom
In spite of the great importance of the matter, if you ask people to define what they mean by freedom, you are likely to encounter definitions that are very questionable. There are many people who think that freedom is 'the ability to do whatever one pleases.' Probably this would be the most

popular definition of freedom, the one that the man in the street would be likely to mention right away if questioned. But if this is what freedom is, then it is something that we do not have, because very often our wishes are conflicting. Suppose that I wish to sit precisely at the place where another person is seated, and suppose he wishes to sit there too. Obviously our two freedoms are conflicting. There is no way in which both of them can be satisfied at the same time.

Some who have recognized this have attempted to adjust the definition by saying, 'Freedom is the ability to do whatever one desires subject to the freedom of another, insofar as it does not interfere with the freedom of another.' But the moment you say 'insofar' you have set limits, and freedom is precisely that which should not be limited if it is to be real.

In any case, even apart from the conflicting interests of the freedom of others, there must be a clear recognition that we simply cannot do whatever we please. Let me say for one moment that I want very much right now to put my finger on the moon. Well, I cannot do that! In order to put my finger on the moon I would have to have a very complex system of rocketry to project me there, and even then it would still take me several days. So I cannot do it at this moment. There are limitations which bind me inevitably and irresistibly. Therefore, if I say that freedom is the ability to do whatever I please, I indicate at once that this is something that man never possesses. It is an illusive goal that cannot ever be attained by anyone.

We need to speak of freedom in a better way, a way that relates it both to the realities of our circumstances and to what God himself has created for us. I would like, therefore, to give a definition which fits better with the pattern that the Bible presents, and then show how this constitutes real freedom and indicate how this freedom relates to law.

True freedom

I would define freedom as *the ability to fulfil one's destiny, to function in terms of one's ultimate goal*. For man the goal is to glorify and serve God in willing obedience. I might say in addition that man's willing obedience involves a responsible and rational process in which man as a rational agent (not a puppet or a robot) is called upon by God to make choices. He is free in that sense. I would like to illustrate that this is what must be understood when we talk about freedom and are conscious of what we are doing rather than just mouthing generalities.

The first illustration is from the inanimate realm, from the realm of mechanics. I will talk in terms of a locomotive or train.

The locomotive can be lent a voice for the purpose of this illustration, and it might easily come forward with a statement like this: 'I am terribly bored in going all the time along precisely the same track. There are many interesting areas to the north and south, and instead of that I am confined strictly to these tracks, seeing the same decrepit houses and the same decrepit factories. I would like to wander around in the hills and meadows and have a chance to be emancipated from this constant following of the tracks.'

Suppose for a moment that we humour the locomotive. We say, 'Okay, go ahead and leave your tracks if you want to.' What would happen? You do not need to be a great train engineer to know what would happen in a situation like this. When the locomotive leaves the tracks it does not wander in pleasant places, in the meadows or hills, along pleasant streams of water. Immediately it ceases completely to operate. You have what is called a derailment. A locomotive is so heavy that it cannot properly proceed on any other surface than its tracks. The locomotive is made for the tracks. It can function only on the tracks. Off the tracks it is inoperative. It achieves nothing and sinks itself in futility. When a locomotive leaves the tracks even for a slight moment what is needed is very heavy apparatus in order to lift it up and bring it back onto the tracks where alone it can operate. Freedom for the train consists in moving along the tracks that have been prepared. Outside of that there is only disaster.

Let us move now to the animal world. I speak of a fish, and here again I will lend the fish a voice in order to illustrate my meaning in relation to freedom. A fish could say, 'I find it very annoying to be always in the water. It is true that on hot days some people view it as a privilege to be in the water, but in my case I am confined to it and find it boring. Once in a while when I jump above the water I can see that there are some other things than water in this world. There are fields, meadows, houses, alluring animals that I would like to get to know better. Why do I have to be confined to water all the time? Water, water everywhere! Why do I have to have that?'

Suppose that we humour the fish in this desire. We say, 'Okay, Mr. Fish, you can get out of the water.' What would happen? You do not need to be a specialist in marine biology to foretell what would happen in a case like this. When a fish is removed from the water it dies. Some of the sturdiest might live as long as two hours, but most of them would not live even that long. The fish has been created to subsist in water. The whole structure of its physiology is related to existence in water. So when a fish moves out of its natural environment, instead of finding liberty, immediately it perishes. Freedom for the fish consists in staying in the water.

Let us now move to the affairs of men. Most of us drive a car, so we will understand the kind of wistfulness that may sometimes come into the heart of a driver when he says, 'Why do I have to be hampered by all these traffic regulations that limit my freedom? Why do I have to stay on the right side of the road? Why can I not wander at ease on this beautiful paved surface that seems to be so ample? And why do I have to bother about those traffic lights that stop me every once in a while? Why do I have to pay attention to those speed limit signs which curtail my freedom – to move as I would like? I would like to drive this car and not have any laws or policemen to limit my ability to enjoy myself behind the wheel.'

Suppose now that the drivers could be humoured in this respect and that suddenly by some decree of the governor all traffic laws were eliminated. What we would have is a monumental traffic jam. There would be accidents. There would be no possibility to foresee anything in relation to using an automobile. You would not know whether a trip would take one hour or whether it would take five hours. So the major purpose of owning a car would be defeated.

Let us go on to the tennis courts. There are some players who might say, 'I find this net very annoying. All my low shots are disannulled and make points for my opponent. Some of my best shots are low shots. Furthermore, the lines that have been drawn on the court are also very annoying. All my strong drives seem to be called out. Why do we have to bother with nets and with lines? Why don't we simply have a chance to bat the ball around without any kind of rules?' Well, there may be some entertainment in batting balls around, but I think that no one who has had very much experience on the courts would fail to say that a few rules go a long way. The real pleasure in tennis consists in playing the game according to the rules of the game.

God's laws

We know this truth in relationship to physical law. We know full well that there are laws that govern our universe and that we are not at liberty to disregard them. If somebody should go to the top of a tower and say, 'I am going to assert my freedom; I am going to float on air now, and I will show you how it is done,' and then launch out without any kind of an aeronautical device that would stop his fall, you know very well what would happen. He would not float on air. The moment he would leave the solid support of the tower the law of gravitation would take hold of him and rush him toward the ground where he would be crushed. A man cannot break the law of gravitation. All he can do is to break himself against it. Anybody who has good sense will acknowledge this and conduct himself accordingly.

What people fail to understand is that the spiritual laws that God has established are equally binding. So we have a lot of people who, knowing full well that they cannot escape physical laws, nevertheless, imagine that in some way they can disregard spiritual laws. They think they can violate the moral laws that God has established at the root of the universe and not bear the consequences. This is folly. Elementary wisdom should teach us that spiritual laws are embedded in the very structure of the universe just as fully as the physical laws are embedded in the physical world. This is God's world, and his will and laws are at the very root of it. Moreover, the laws of God do not represent a painful and tyrannical imposition which God places upon people who are legitimately opposed to them. They represent the lines of force of the universe that God has created, and so point the way to true freedom. To disregard the laws of God is not to achieve freedom; it is to sink into futility. It is to break oneself against the structure of the world in which we live.

A spiritual map
Some people disregard the law that we are to love our neighbour as ourselves. They entertain thoughts of hatred in their hearts. They live for revenge. They plot it. Whom do they harm by this? Well, sometimes they do hurt the people they want to harm; that is true. But supremely they harm

themselves. They are doing something bad for the human constitution. Doctors tell us that about fifty per cent of the people that come for treatment are not sick because of organic defects that spoil their bodies but because of some mental attitude that actually erodes their health. Continued feelings of hatred do something bad for the digestive system; people may get ulcers from it. There are people who get ulcers from worry.

The Scripture also tells us that God has established laws for our sexual behaviour. There are people who say, 'This business of sex in marriage is antiquated. That's 'old hat.' Now we are liberated. We understand what human sexuality is all about, and the point is to enjoy any part of it that we can in any way that we wish.' But when they do that they work havoc in their lives. God says, 'Thou shalt not commit adultery.' They disregard his law, but they do not break it; they break themselves against it. So we have people who are discontented, distraught, who strew with wreckage the highways of this world. We simply cannot disregard with impunity what God has ordered.

Think of it in terms of selfishness. God has said that we must not put ourselves at the centre of the universe. God must be the centre. But people say, 'Well, I am interested in myself.' And what happens? Inevitably they ruin their relationship with their fellowmen. Instead of having the kind of company and joy that they could perhaps anticipate from their fellowmen, they become undesirable people. It is very boring and tiring to keep on serving somebody who is constantly serving himself. So the selfish person makes a void around himself. Instead of having more and more friends, he has fewer and fewer, until finally he seems to get what he was wanting: he gets himself! And that is not a big bargain!

The law of God is written deep in the structure of the universe. We cannot break it, but we can break ourselves on it. When we choose to disobey it that is exactly what we do. We break ourselves against the lines of force of the universe which God has created.

It is right to oppose legalism, because legalism represents an attitude of rigid adherence to law, not for the purpose of the law, but merely for the sake of following regulations. That is unfortunate. But the law, far from being a burden upon us, is actually an expression of the grace of God. It is through grace that God has been pleased to reveal the lines of structure of the world so that we may enjoy lives of success and blessing in obedience to them. I have never yet seen a motorist who felt that it was an imposition on him to receive a road map. Most motorists that I know are very happy when they have a good road map, because it shows them where they should go and what course they should take. The law of God is a road map which shows us how to guide ourselves in this world. So freedom for man does not consist in the ability to disregard the law or commandment of God. Freedom for man resides precisely in the opposite ability – in obedience – because it is then only that he can achieve his destiny.

The source of freedom
Unfortunately, we do not have this freedom because, as the Lord Jesus Christ said, 'Everyone who sins is a slave to sin' (John 8:34). We may well recognize that freedom is to be found in obeying the law of God, but we know that we disobey. And the Scripture makes it plain that we have lost our ability to adhere constantly and permanently to the law of God in perfect obedience. Ever since Adam and Eve fell in paradise, the whole of mankind by natural generation is encompassed in a terrible rebellion, corruption, and slavery in which, even in spite of some desires that we may have from time to time to do what is right, we are constantly carried along. So we sigh deeply in our heart, 'What a wretched man

I am! Who will rescue me?' (Rom. 7:24). 'How shall I get that emancipation? How shall I get freedom?' We say, 'Give me liberty, because I am already encompassed in death.'

It is here that the gospel comes in. For when we understand our predicament and recognize our plight, then we hear the Lord Jesus Christ who says to us, 'If the Son sets you free, you will be free indeed' (John 8:36). This is a proclamation of authentic freedom, not some kind of superficial or merely political freedom, but freedom that is real – 'You shall be *really* free.' And this is what God in his mercy does, for the Lord Jesus Christ provides for us a *new nature*. Instead of being born of the flesh, we are born from above. We are born of the Spirit (John 3:5), by the mighty seed of the Word of God (1 Pet. 1:23). By this rebirth the Spirit of God reorients our lives. Lives that have been distorted and disrupted by sin now receive a new orientation from God himself by which they are related to his divine purpose.

Moreover, the Lord Jesus Christ provides a *new record* for us. Our old record is one that leads only to condemnation. As the prayer of confession of Geneva says it: 'Lord, we acknowledge and confess before your holy majesty that we are miserable sinners, born in iniquity, inclined unto evil, incapable of doing by ourselves any good, and who transgress every day in several ways your holy commandment. Wherefore we deserve, by your just judgment, condemnation and death.' That is our predicament. And it does not help to say, 'But I have observed some of the commandments,' because the Lord makes plain that whoever disobeys even one commandment is guilty of all before the law (James 2:10, 11). In order to be cast into prison it is not necessary that you should have committed every kind of crime there is. One is enough. But the Lord provides a new record because he has assumed the burden of our sins. He has taken our sins in his body on the cross (1 Pet. 2:24). He has paid the full penalty required by the law and awesome justice of God in order that we might be freed from the eternal consequences of our sins. He has covered us with the immaculate record of his own righteousness so that in the words of the apostle Paul 'There is, therefore, now no condemnation to them who are in Christ Jesus' (Rom. 8:1).

The redemption of Jesus Christ brings in *new power:* new power to deal with the evil tendencies that we find within us, new power to achieve victory, new power to break the various chains of evil that may hamper and disfigure our lives. 'Just as you used to offer the parts of your body in slavery to impurity and to ever increasing wickedness;' says the apostle Paul, 'so now offer them in slavery to righteousness and holiness. When you were slaves to sin, you were free from the control of righteousness. What benefit did you reap at that time from the things you are ashamed of? Those things result in death! But now that you have been set free from sin and have become slaves to God, the benefit you reap leads to holiness and the result is eternal life. For the wages of sin is death, but the gift of God is eternal life through Christ Jesus our Lord' (Rom. 6:19-23).

What a wonderful redemption, what a wonderful liberation Christ has brought into this world plunged in the bondage and slavery of sin!

13

Prayer: The Prelude to Revival

God's sovereignty embraces absolutely everything. That includes prayer and preaching. That might seem obvious enough. But perhaps you have met people who think we should have a motto which goes like this: 'You ought to pray like a Calvinist and preach like an Arminian.' That is, pray as if everything depended upon God and preach as if everything depended on men. I would like to suggest a change in this formula which will improve it by fifty percent: 'You ought to pray like a Calvinist and preach like a Calvinist.' Do not pray *as if* everything depended on God. Pray because everything depends on God. (There is no good reason to have an 'as if' in that motto, because things do depend on God. He is the one who sovereignly ordains and blesses.) Then preach like a Calvinist too, because there too the results depend on God. Neither prayer nor preaching is an activity in which we suddenly take leave of the doctrine of God's sovereignty.

This is especially true of prayer for revival. Lasting revival should be grounded in prayer, because in prayer we acknowledge God's sovereignty. God alone is the one who can dispense revival. So revival is not something that is within the reach of human beings. It is something God alone can provide. Hence the crying need for prayer.

What does prayer change?
When we consider prayer there are questions which often are disturbing to the minds of some people. The first question

is: Do you think that you can really change the mind of God? Can prayer make God modify his sovereign plan? There are people who feel that unless you are prepared to say this, there is no great value in prayer. I do not know what your particular idea on this subject may be, but I would like to say that if you believe you can change the mind of God through prayer, I hope you are using some discretion. If that is the power you have, it is certainly a most dangerous thing. Surely God does not need our counsel in order to set up what is desirable. Surely God, whose knowledge penetrates all minds and hearts, does not need to have us intervene to tell him what he ought to do. The thought that we are changing the mind of God by our prayers is a terrifying conception.

I will be frank to confess, if I really thought I could change the mind of God by praying, I would abstain. Because I would have to say, 'How can I presume, with the limitations of my own mind and the corruptions of my own heart – how can I presume to interfere in the counsels of the Almighty?' It is almost as if you were to introduce somebody who is utterly ignorant of electronics to a weapons plant in which, by pushing certain buttons, one might precipitate an explosion. You say, 'Go ahead and push buttons. Never mind what happens.' Oh, no! There is comfort for the child of God in being assured that our prayers will not change God's mind. This is not what is involved in prayer, and we are not in danger of precipitating explosions by some rash desire on our part.

But then people say, 'If you cannot change God's mind, what is the point of praying? If prayer does not change things, prayer is worthless.'

Here you have perhaps noticed that I have changed the formula. I did not say, 'change the mind of God,' but 'change things.' I never said that prayer does not change things. Prayer does change things, but it does not change the mind of God. The reason prayer changes things but does not change God is that he has appointed prayer as an effectual means for accomplishing his own purpose. This effectual means is essential for this accomplishment. When we have a right understanding of the sovereignty of God we recognize that God has established a plan in which not only the effects but also the causes are ordained. We cannot disconnect the causes from the effects or the effects from the causes.

For example, I lift a book in your sight. Because the book has risen in the air, I am in a position to say, 'God has ordained that it should get to this particular place.' He must have ordained it because that is where the book is. But notice, God did not ordain for the book to rise all by itself. He ordained that it should rise at the end of my hand. He ordained that I should have strength in my arm to lift it. He ordained that I should choose this particular book in order to illustrate this particular point. There is a connection between the book rising and the subject I wish to develop. All these things are tied up together. If there were no lecture, there would be no point in illustrating the power of second causes. If there were no desire to illustrate the power of second causes, my hand would have remained at my side. If my hand had remained at my side, the book would not have risen. I think we can argue in this way.

God, however, ordained that there should be this occasion, that there should be a desire to show the correlation of causes and effects in his sovereign plan, that this particular illustration should come to my mind and that I should implement it by the strength that he has given me. One cannot say, 'If you hadn't touched it, it would have risen anyway,' because God did not ordain that it should rise anyway. He ordained that it should rise through my hand.

That is exactly the case with prayer. Prayer is an effectual secondary cause that God has related to the effects involved. Just as the activity of human beings on earth is related to the effects that are produced, just as the book rising is related to the hand lifting, so are the effects of prayer related to the prayer that is offered. So although prayer does not change the mind of God, it does change things. God has appointed change through prayer, even though the way in which the cause is related to the effect is not perfectly clear to us.

The fact that the way this happens is not clear does not give us ground for denying the relationship. We pray for healing. If God provides healing, we cannot say, 'There would have been healing whether I prayed or not; I would have gotten well anyway.' God provided healing in relation to prayer.

We pray for an increase in the knowledge of God and earnestness in his service. If God is pleased to bless our lives in this way, we cannot say, 'This would have happened whether I prayed or not.' God provides his blessing in relation to the prayer.

We pray for the salvation of someone we love, someone God has placed on our hearts to intercede and plead for. That person is born again by the work of the Holy Spirit. But we cannot say, 'This would have happened whether I prayed or not.' It is related to our prayers. God, who has appointed the salvation, has also appointed prayer as the means to that salvation. We cannot omit any link in that chain and say that the chain will exist whether the link is there or not.

A final question is: How can I pray if I do not see how prayer works? That is not a wise way of handling the matter, since it is God who tells us that prayer is part of his plan for us. It is not necessary that we should have an understanding of the ways in which God's purposes are implemented. God has put this means at our disposal. He encourages us to pray. In 2 Chronicles 7:14 he says, 'If my people, who are called by my name, will humble themselves and pray and seek my face and turn from their wicked ways, then will I hear from heaven and will forgive their sin and will heal their land.' To insist that we must have an understanding of how this works is a very unreasonable attitude.

Even in affairs of daily life we do not have this attitude. I am sure you have used a touch-system telephone. Do you understand how it works? Do you have that consummate knowledge of communications to know exactly what goes on when you press those little buttons? Do you know how those numbers are changed into binary code and used to track down the particular telephone you wish to call? Experts may understand this. But I must say, so far as I am concerned, when I am calling I do not think of any of those things. I just pick up the phone and touch the buttons. I do not worry about how this happens. I am only interested in whom I am going to reach and what I will say.

It is the same with prayer. We do not have to know how it works. It is enough to know that it does work. Prayer is part of God's sovereign plan and is an effectual means by which we can share with God in the fulfilment of that plan. When we pray we are co-operating, we are working together with God in the work to which in his own mercy he has been pleased to call us.

Since prayer is part of God's plan, we are not forcing God's hand at any time by praying. We are not intruding our own will in a way that is disagreeable or uncomfortable to God. We do not need to fear that we are pushing buttons about which we know nothing, which might bring disaster on ourselves and others. We are praying in line with the great purposes of God. Without prayer there are many things that would be different. It is by virtue of prayer that they are what God has planned them to be.

Prayer and revival

In Scripture, prayer is presented as a prerequisite for revival. It is a prelude. If you study the history of revivals, you will find that they are best documented not only in their effects but also in their preparatory prayer periods. This was true of the revivals in New England under the ministry of Jonathan Edwards. It was true in the revivals in Wales under Evan Roberts. It was true of the revivals under the ministry of Charles Grandison Finney in the United States. Revival that is worthwhile is bathed in prayer. When he wants a revival God is pleased to lead his people to pray that revival might be forthcoming.

The prayer that leads to revival must be *believing* prayer. This is the point the apostle James makes in his letter (James 1:5-7). When we come to the Lord we must come with expectation that he is able and will do great things. If we come vacillating, wondering whether God is able to accomplish anything, whether the situation is really so desperate that even God cannot touch it, then obviously our prayer is lacking in fervency. We are just going through the motions, as it were. We are not really praying.

God wants us to come to him in faith. Indeed, prayer is an exercise of faith in which we are steeped in the supreme greatness and ability of God and have our eyes fixed on the majesty of his purpose and the superlative quality of his resources. Nothing is impossible for our God. Our God is able to move mountains. He is able to transform hearts, break resistances, reach out even underneath the conscious life of people to transform them. So we should never say, 'Here is somebody beyond God's reach. The hardness of heart is so great, the wickedness of life is so manifest, that this cannot possibly be a candidate for acceptance into the kingdom of God. We might as well give up on this person.'

In spite of the fact that the early church had seen God do

many great things, it undoubtedly thought this way about
Paul. The early Christians thought, 'This one is lost. There is
no way God will bring Paul into the kingdom. He is a
persecutor, an enemy, an opponent. There is no hope for him.'
When Paul tried to join the church, they gave him the cold
shoulder (Acts 9:26). They said, 'We can't trust this man. He
will be spying on us and then use his knowledge to annihilate
the church.' It took Barnabas to reason, 'God saved me; maybe
he can save Paul too.' He went close to Paul and befriended
him at great danger to himself. He made sure that Paul truly
was a child of God. Then he brought him to the apostles (Acts
9:27). We too might think, 'What less likely a candidate for
election than Paul!' Yet God was pleased to reach him and
change him. God made him the great apostle of the Gentiles,
the benefit of whose ministry is still with us to this day.

We need believing prayer, prayer that does not concentrate
on the obstacles. We must not say, 'He is hopeless' or 'Our
country has gone to the dogs' or 'Our church has gone liberal.'
Prayer must recognize that God is all-powerful and can do
wonders. If anybody prays and does not believe, that one is
unstable (James 1:6, 7). He cannot expect anything. But if
we come with faith, accepting the reality of the power of
God, then we will experience that effective prayer changes
things in keeping with God's purpose.

If it be God's will

The second characteristic of the prayer that brings revival is
submission. It must be *submissive* prayer. That is, we must
be prepared to submit our own ideas, aims and ambitions to
the sovereign God. We must not intrude with our outlook,
pressing it on God, as it were. Rather, we must come with a
desire to understand God's outlook and subordinate our
desires to what he has ordained.

Some people say, 'That kind of prayer is not really

effective. If you start by saying, "If it be your will...," you are attempting to give God a way out in case he is not going to do it. You are not believing.' That is not the point at all. We do not need to give God a way out. God does not need a way out. What we are doing when we say, 'If it is your will....' is articulating the principle that we are not telling God what should be done but are actually identifying with his purpose and asking to work together with him in fulfilment of that purpose.

We have a moving example of this kind of prayer on the lips of our Lord himself. In Gethsemane he said, 'If it is possible.... Yet not as I will, but as you will' (Matt. 26:39). This is mysterious to us, for it indicates that at that point of his human consciousness our Lord was left in suspense as to what the will of God was. 'Not as I will, but as you will.' That is the condition of effective prayer: that we should be willing to accept what God has ordained in order that his purpose might be accomplished.

Sometimes it is hard for us to pray that way, because our will is so strong and our understanding of what God should want is so clear that we do not even feel like saying, 'Your will be done.' When we pray for revival especially we say, 'We do not need to introduce conditional clauses. The very fact that God leads us to prayer is an indication that he wills that some form of revival should come.' Still, the very essence of a consecrated prayer is that it should be in keeping with the will of God.

This is what is meant by praying in the name of Jesus. To pray in the name of Christ is not simply to have a little addition to your prayer, in which you use those words almost as a magical formula to ensure success. To pray in the name of Christ is to identify yourself with Christ, with his aims, his purposes, his ministry. It is to say, 'I am with Jesus. I am for him and his purposes.' The one who prays in the name of

Jesus does not need to fear disappointments, because unity with the purpose of God protects him from that. There is a submission to God which acknowledges with gratitude the way in which God is pleased to answer.

This prayer must be God-centred. It must relate itself to God's glory rather than to our private desires. Of course, God permits us to present our private desires as well. There is nothing wrong in asking God to give us good weather for mountain climbing if good weather is important for it. But here again, it would be wise to say, 'If it be your will,' because there are also people, such as farmers, who need rain. Since the desire of the mountaineer may conflict with the desire of the farmer, it would be good for both of them to be submitted to whatever God is pleased to send. God permits us to present our desires. But we must have a supreme desire, especially in the prayer for revival, to see the glory of God manifested.

Some of the most effective prayers in Scripture do this. They are even argumentative at this point. Think of the prayer of Abraham when he prayed for Sodom and Gomorrah. He argued with God, saying, 'Is it right for you to destroy those cities if fifty…forty-five…forty…thirty…twenty…ten righteous people live there?' (Gen. 18:24-33). God blessed that prayer. So we can say that if Lot and his family were saved, it was because of the faithful intercession of Abraham, who did not relent, even though in the end the number he cited was not sufficiently small to warrant salvation of the wicked cities.

Think of the prayer of Moses who argued, 'If you destroy your people, what will happen to your name? Your glory is at stake. Don't do it' (Exod. 32:11-13). God blessed that glorious intercessory prayer of Moses, who disregarded his personal ambition in order to identify with the purposes of God.

A prayer for revival should be centred, not in the desire

that we should have more money for our church (because there will be more people coming), nor that there should be a new vitality in our denomination (as compared with other denominations), nor that any other of our human desires and ambitions should be satisfied, but rather that the glory of God might be manifested. We should pray that his name might be exalted, that his kingdom might be made evident, that his glorious reign might be established even more widely in the hearts of men and women.

Do not give up

Our prayer must be *persistent*. The Scripture emphasizes that we ought not easily to be discouraged in prayer (Luke 18:1). If we do not receive at once the answer we are looking for, we ought not to reason, 'Well, God just doesn't want me to have that; I guess I'll give up.' There are people who have been wonderfully persistent in prayer for husbands or wives, children or parents – and God has blessed their persistence. Do not give up too soon. Do not conclude too rapidly that God is uninterested. So long as you have a burden on your heart, keep praying.

In the church in which I am a member there is a man who has moved me profoundly in this respect. It is a wonderful church now. We have a preacher who is a wonderful expositor of the Word of God. I never attend a service there at which my soul is not blessed. But some forty years ago this church was exceedingly small – there were about ten or twelve people on a Sunday morning – and it was passing through a veritable desert from the point of view of biblical ministry. I understand that at one time one of the pastors was actually a practising Christian Scientist. Throughout this bleak period this man, Deacon George Day, was praying. He did not say, 'This church gives me nothing. There is nothing to be expected here, nothing to be hoped. I am going to find another fellowship that will be more fruitful for me.' No! This man said, 'This is my church. I am not going to give up. Since I do not get any spiritual nurture from the sermons, I will get it from the Bible directly. I will attend some other meetings in other places. But I am still going to be in my own church on Sunday morning, and I am going to pray for this ministry.' Deacon Day kept praying for that church for years. Now he is an old man, more than eighty. There is hardly any strength left in his body. When he can come to church he uses an earphone, because he is very deaf. But there is joy in his heart which moves one to tears. Whenever I see Deacon Day I see the power of God to answer persistent prayer. I see a warrior who did not allow himself to be defeated but who stayed at his post, pleading for his church and asking God's blessing upon it.

Pray and work also

Finally, the prayer that leads to revival must be *consistent* prayer in which we are prepared also to do what we can to achieve what we are asking. If we pray for the conversion of our loved ones, somehow we must give our witness too. We must witness by life and words, when they can be effectually presented. If we pray for revival, we must be prepared to open our hearts so that God may revive them. We ought never to take prayer as a means of avoiding the actions God challenges us to.

My father had an experience which I would like to relate in closing. As a young minister he had been an assistant in a large church which had only had two pastors in fifty years, one ministry of fifty years followed by another of fifty years. But after having been in that church, my father became pastor of a very small church in a little village in southern France. The prayer meeting was on Wednesday evening, and there was usually a very limited attendance. One Wednesday there was a frightful storm. The wind was blowing. Rain was falling in buckets. My father thought, 'There is not going to be anybody at the prayer meeting tonight. If I go, I will only drench myself. I might as well stay at home.' My father was very interested in Hebrew and was studying the song of Deborah in the Book of Judges. The temptation was great to stay in his cosy home and deal with that.

As my father was wrestling with this, there came to his memory a sermon given at the time of his ordination. It was on the passage which says, 'Go out and constrain them to come in' (Luke 14:23). Most of the time we think about the expression 'constrain them to come in.' But on this occasion the preacher had focused on the phrase, 'Go out.' He had said, '"Go out" means to reach out for people; it means, do not stay in the cosiness of your study. You must go out and reach out.' While the gales were blowing and the wind was hitting the windows, my father remembered that and concluded, 'Well, I guess God wants me to go out. I do not expect many people. I do not expect very much of anything at this prayer meeting. But if God has told me to go out, I will go out and speak at the prayer meeting.' This was the meeting in which revival started in his church!

Prayer is the prelude to revival. Do you want revival? Then be prepared to pray. 'If my people, who are called by my name, will humble themselves and pray ....then will I hear from heaven and will forgive their sins and will heal their land' (2 Chron. 7:14).

14

The Final Judgment

The topic of God's judgment is rarely popular. Certainly, when the apostle Paul spoke about judgment, he did not have very much success. He preached on judgment at Athens; but when he began to speak about the resurrection and the judgment to come, the people interrupted him and refused to let him continue. Later in Acts, we find Paul facing Felix, a governor, again speaking about righteousness, self-control (something Felix lacked) and judgment to come. Felix was afraid and said, 'That's enough for now. You may leave. When I find it convenient, I will send for you' (Acts 24:25). But he never did.

Yet, God's final judgment is essential for the display of his glory. How could a God whose eyes are too pure to look upon evil allow such evil to go unpunished? Could he permit there to be no difference at the end of the day between the righteous and the wicked? If we are concerned for God's glory, we will reflect on the final judgment with both hope and seriousness.

A dominant doctrine

I begin by saying that the idea of a future judgment by God is strongly emphasized in Scripture. One Hebrew root that we translate 'judge' or 'judgment' occurs more than two hundred times in the Old Testament There are even sixty-five verses spoken by Jesus that deal with the subject of judgment, and if you add in verses on 'punishment' there are at least a hundred more. We only have about 1,800 to 1,900 verses from Jesus' own lips. So a sizable percentage of these concern judgment.

I have not attempted to count how often Jesus speaks about love, but I have the impression that he may have spoken more often about judgment than he spoke about love, even though, naturally enough, we are immensely concerned and grateful for what he has to tell us about the subject.

So this is not some minor feature of the Word of God that only some specialists might be interested in. This is an issue that looms large on the pages of Holy Writ.

People have an aversion to this topic. Many who deal with it say at some point or another, 'It is just not fashionable to speak about this nowadays.' People are not impressed by judgment, as they used to be in the eighteenth century, when Jonathan Edwards could preach a sermon like 'Sinners in the Hands of an Angry God' and cause his audience to tremble. But judgment is nevertheless a reality and a strong theme in the Bible.

Need for judgment
The idea of judgment, far from distasteful, ought to be recognized by any right thinking woman or man as essential for the proper understanding of life and for a wholesome world-and-life view. In Psalm 73:2-11 Asaph says,

> But as for me my feet had almost slipped;
> I had nearly lost my foothold.
> For I envied the arrogant
> when I saw the prosperity of the wicked.
> They have no struggles;
> their bodies are healthy and strong.
> They are free from the burdens common to man;
> they are not plagued by human ills.
> Therefore pride is their necklace;
> they clothe themselves with violence.

From their callous hearts comes iniquity;
the evil conceits of their minds know no limits.
They scoff, and speak with malice;
 in their arrogance they threaten oppression.
Their mouths lay claim to heaven,
and their tongues take possession of the earth.
Therefore their people turn to them
and drink up waters in abundance.
They say, 'How can God know?
 Does the Most High have knowledge?'

This is what the wicked are like. This is a description of
the Mafia and of many other focal points of evil. If this life
ends with the moment of death and there is nothing beyond,
then we are left with a picture that is absolutely disconcerting.
We are left with such a picture that probably people of the
greatest wisdom would say, 'Let us be done with it as quickly
as possible and commit suicide. Life doesn't mean anything.
We might as well take our leave as early as we can.'

If the people who engineered the holocaust are to be
reduced to powder in no worse way than the people they
burned in the gas chambers, we can rightly protest: 'What
kind of a world are we living in anyway?' How can we be
reconciled with such flagrant injustice? How can we accept
that the wicked do not meet their proper punishment? How
can we think that God is in control – or even that there is a
God – if justice does not ultimately prevail?

Therefore even though the thought of judgment is
threatening to us, there is still great hope in judgment. Without
judgment humanity is undone and our world makes no sense
whatever. Judgment is the only hope we have that this world
is not going topsy-turvy without any kind of direction, that it
is not running along into the abyss like a great express train
without rails.

Do you know the story of the palace of Sans Souci near
Berlin? The great Prussian conqueror Frederick had plans

for building a castle and had purchased land for it. But there was one farmer who just did not want to sell his property. The king went to see this man to try to persuade him to release his property, perhaps making a certain profit on it, but at least not blocking the emperor's plans simply because he wanted to stay on his farm. The king found him in the fields and said, 'I am Frederick. I want to buy your farm. Do you realize that in refusing to sell your land you are blocking my plans?'

The man replied, 'I am not interested in selling. It is not because I want to block your plans, but this is my farm. I received it from my parents; I love it and I don't want to sell it.'

The king said, 'Do you know that if I wanted to I could compel you to sell it?'

The farmer said, 'No, you cannot. There are judges in Berlin who would stop you.'

Frederick had the good sense to be very happy about this answer, because he felt it was a compliment to his country. There were judges in Berlin who would be prepared to override the will of the king in order to maintain the rights of the individual citizen. He decided to change his plans. He built his castle around this farm, and the farm became an exhibit of the fact that this was a country where justice was safeguarded and where even the king could not place himself above the law.

When we think about justice and judgment in our world we have grounds for hope. For we know that this world has not simply gone topsy-turvy. We know that God has not lost control. We know that he keeps records of everything, and that in the end 'the Judge of all the earth will do right' (Gen. 18:25). If this were not the very basis of our whole approach to life, we would flounder, discouraged and broken, in utter futility.

Judgment now

The judgment of God is made apparent in a number of ways even while we live. God has ordained that many people do not have to wait until they fall under the judgment of God by some special calamity but rather that they judge themselves. The Gospel of John makes this very plain. It says, 'This is the verdict: Light has come into the world, and men loved darkness instead of light because their deeds were evil' (John 3:19). So they have judged themselves.

Leon Morris, in his fine little book *The Biblical Doctrine of Judgment*, calls attention to the case of Judas who, he says, sold *himself* for thirty pieces of silver, not Christ. Morris means that judgment is a present reality in that we bear judgment against ourselves: That is part of the order God has established. We are not like a herd of cattle that is simply being prodded toward an uncertain end or catastrophe. We are beings God has endowed with a sense of right and wrong. We know that we must do right and flee from wrong. When we disobey we render judgment against ourselves. We do not even have to have a special occasion at the end in order to mark this.

The Bible does not offer hope of some second chance for us after death. Now is the time in which the issues of life and death must be faced. We cannot postpone our decisions, saying, 'We'll consider that later' or 'I have received so little information that God surely could not condemn me.' The whole race is under the righteous condemnation of God, and each one of us individually amply merits a just and proper condemnation. This remains somewhat private since there is no public declaration of our end. Only God can tell who goes to hell and who to heaven. So it is necessary that the judicial and proper order of God's righteousness be manifested. God shows us in Scripture, particularly in Revelation 20 (which describes the judgment of the great white throne), that he has appointed a day in which he will cause every rational being to appear before him to give an account, and justice will be rendered.

Man's judgment, God's judgment

When we examine Scripture we find that there is a contrast between what happens at the judgment seat of God and Christ, and what can happen in the administration of justice on this earth.

I do not want to defame the administration of justice. I feel that justice on the human level is important in any political arrangement. I believe that in the United States of America there is a wonderful system of justice administered at the local, state and Supreme Court levels. But in spite of serious efforts to provide justice in civilized nations like the United States, there are nevertheless some fearful miscarriages of justice. There are ways in which our courts are, I think, rightly subject to criticism. One of the major criticisms is that sometimes the rights of offenders are so carefully preserved that victims are left without rights. People who do evil can invoke all kinds of technicalities, but the people who have been maimed and robbed, or who have lost their loved ones, seem to find very little support in the law. There is little to help them, little to assuage their grief, very little to compensate them for their losses. Some of them are rightly outraged.

The judgment seat of God will have none of these frailties.

To start with, there will be *no defaulting*. All people, great and small, will be there. Nobody will be able to find a refuge in Argentina to escape being visited by God's judgment. There will be no clefts in any rock to hide anybody. There will be people who will say, 'Mountains, fall on us! We'd sooner be crushed by a mountain than face the judgment.' But the mountains will not obey. The mountains will remain where they are, and these people will have to face God. Every single human being that has ever lived or will ever live will be there, even without the need of any kind of special policeman to bring them manacled to court. There will be no escape.

There will be *no plea-bargaining* with God. Plea-bargaining is a device by which people who have committed a more grievous crime hope to have a lesser punishment by sparing the state a certain amount of expense and risk in prosecuting them. But with God there is no plea-bargaining. God knows exactly what every person has done, said and thought. Everybody will have to answer for his or her deeds precisely.

There will be *no need of prosecutors*. A prosecutor is a person who has to develop a case in order that the matter may be adjudicated with propriety. The prosecutor must prove beyond reasonable doubt that the accused person is in fact guilty. There will be no prosecutor at the great white throne, because God has video tapes which do not have eighteen and a half minutes missing anywhere. They are absolutely complete. There is no need to make a case, because the case is in the mind of God, who knows all, sees all, weighs all, and who has a perfect understanding of every mitigating circumstance and every range of influence that has come upon a person, and who is prepared on his own to provide an entirely proper verdict.

There will be *no lawyers for the defence*. Lawyers plead technicalities, and some of them manage to rescue clear-cut scoundrels from the punishment they deserve. God knows exactly what the score is, and there will be no way in which anybody can retard his justice.

There will be *no false witnesses* in the judgment. God does not need witnesses, because he has all the facts at his fingertips.

There will be *no jury*, because there is no danger that God could be partial or be bribed in favour of somebody who managed to get to him. God, the Judge of all the earth, will do right. He does not need any help, any counsel, any friend of the court to help him reach the right verdict. The verdict will be right in every case.

There will *be no postponements*. The judgment will be the last day; the matter will be settled.

There will be *no suspended sentences*. The sentence that will be rendered will be implemented immediately, as Revelation 20 shows us.

There will be *no appeals*, because there are no grounds on which anybody can possibly appeal against God's decision. It will be as just and righteous as God himself is just and righteous.

There will be *no paroles*, because the decision of God is irrevocable.

There will be *no pardons*.

In human courts these things are useful to safeguard the rights of innocent persons who could otherwise be condemned unjustly. But these matters will not be present in the judgment of God. The judgment of God will be decisive, eternal, irrevocable. It will condemn us all. There is not a single human being, save our Lord Jesus Christ, who, appearing before the judgment seat of God, can say, 'I have done absolutely everything you had a right to ask of me to do. I am free of all fault.' Human beings will be declared guilty. God will be vindicated.

Christ bore our judgment

If that does not impress you, I invite you to consider how this judgment was, in fact, administered even before the last days. On his knees, with his face in the dirt, is the Son of God himself. There is blood on his brow, and he is pleading with the Father: 'Father, if it is possible, may this cup be taken from me. Yet not as I wilt but as you will' (Matt 26:39). This is the one occasion in his life on which Jesus actually asked the help of his disciples. He pleaded with them to stay awake with him and support him with their prayers. But he rose and found them asleep. 'Could you men not keep watch with me for one hour?' he asked (v. 40). Then he returned and prayed again, 'If it is not possible for this cup to be taken away unless I drink it, may your will be done' (v. 42).

What was it that caused the Lord Jesus Christ to cringe in the presence of suffering? Surely, it is not that he was afraid that he would have pain on the cross. It is perfectly obvious when you read the Gospels that when he was on the cross he kept control better than the people around him. In fact the remarkable thing is that he was calm amid the nervousness and erratic behaviour of others. Our Lord was not afraid that somehow people would hurt him. The cup of which he was speaking was the bitter cup of our sins which, like a vast horrible sewer, was being poured out upon his clean and perfect soul. Even though he had come for this hour, even though he knew that the cup could not pass away if he was to redeem his people, he had a natural desire to avoid this frightful ordeal.

Less than twenty-four hours later, when he was on the cross, the sun suddenly hid its light and there was darkness on the earth. The disciples heard a cry of such desperation, such intense sorrow that they could not even put it in another language. They gave it in the very form in which they heard it: *'Eloi, Eloi, lama sabachthani?'* which means, 'My God, my God, why have you forsaken me?' (Matt 27:46). Here was the Lord in our place to bear our judgment.

This is a foretaste of what the last judgment will be. How can you escape it, if you neglect so great salvation? My dear friends, how can you hope to stand up in the presence of God in the day of judgment unless you are covered by Jesus Christ? In that day only those who are in Christ will be forgiven. All others will have to hear those fateful and tragic words: 'Away from me, all you evildoers' (Luke 13:27). Only in the cross may we hide our souls from the wrath to come.

May God admonish us by the thought of judgment and may he make us eager to find the refuge he has provided. Shall not the Judge of all the earth do right? Yes, he certainly shall do right. He did right in Jesus Christ, not sparing his only Son but delivering him to death so we might be saved.

Christian Focus Publications publishes biblically accurate books for adults and children. The books in the adult range are published in three imprints.

Christian Heritage contains classic writings from the past.

Christian Focus contains popular works including biographies, commentaries, doctrine, and Christian living.

Mentor focuses on books written at a level suitable for Bible College and seminary students, pastors, and others; the imprint includes commentaries, doctrinal studies, examination of current issues, and church history.

For a free catalogue of all our titles, please write to

Christian Focus Publications, Ltd
Geanies House, Fearn,
Ross-shire, IV20 1TW, Great Britain

For details of our titles visit us on our website

http://www.christianfocus.com